What read

∽

"Congratulations! Your work is very important, as my past life work has helped me immensely." With love, Dr. Terry Cole-Whittaker

"Thank you for your wonderful work! Through you passes love, truth, acceptance, and of course, Spirit. I wanted to read it slow and saver the work of a great writer – someone who writes so that all may comprehend – but I gobbled up all the words so greedily. I was humbled by each person's courage to pursue personal truth and integrity." – K.S., Renton, WA

"I was blessed to have been given your book Soul Contracts! I am still wrestling with the after affects of my abortion that I had twenty-seven years ago. I need to put closure on this. I hope you audiotape will lead me closer. Thank you." – D.O. Chelmsford, MA

"I just finished reading Soul Contracts and I could hardly put it down! This book really spoke to me." – D.T., Chapel Hill, N.C.

"I like your book and thank you for writing it. I especially like the way it is written. It flows from within the spirit and honors each person's experiences. It is rare to find a book that is soul full and compassionate and supports 'not knowing the truth' but going on adventures of discovery - S.E., Issaquah, WA

"Thank you for writing such a beautiful and inspiring book!" –E.R., Seattle, WA

"I really enjoyed reading Soul Contracts – especially: The Importance of Forgiveness." –S.L., Seattle, WA

"I want to thank you for writing the book Soul Contracts. It has helped me to understand so much of what is happening in my life

right now! It is also gives me great hope for healing, for myself as well as for my soon to be ex-husband." -I.B., Arlington, MA

"In this book, Linda Baker uses personal accounts of her work with individuals to illustrate not only the human capacity to transform but also the invisible realm which facilitates these transformations. As a hypnotherapist she has incredible insight and as a writer has a talent to communicate what she has learned about soul contracts through her many years of practice. I found this book very insightful and interesting." – L.J., Seattle, WA

"I am almost finished with your book Soul Contracts and I find it fascinating, illuminating and helpful." -K.W., Harvard University, MA

"I am a Labor & Delivery nurse and in L&D we find ourselves offering abortions for both fetal demise and fetal anomalies. It is always hugely traumatic for these women and I find myself wondering what we, as nurses, can do to help these women cope with the profound sadness they experience. Thank you for your excellent book and tape." – D.G., Post Falls, Idaho

Soul Contracts

How They Affect Your Life and Your Relationships - Past life Therapy to Change Your Present Life

New 2010 Edition

Linda Baker R.N.; C.H.T.

Author of *The Bridge Between Worlds*

iUniverse, Inc.
New York   Bloomington

Soul Contracts
How They Affect Your Life and Your Relationships - Past life
Therapy to Change Your Present Life

iUniverse books may be ordered through booksellers or by contacting:

iUniverse
1663 Liberty Drive
Bloomington, IN 47403
www.iuniverse.com
1-800-Authors (1-800-288-4677)

*Because of the dynamic nature of the Internet, any Web addresses or links contained in
this book may have changed since publication and may no longer be valid. The views
expressed in this work are solely those of the author and do not necessarily reflect the
views of the publisher, and the publisher hereby disclaims any responsibility for them.*

ISBN: 978-1-4502-3710-9 (sc)
ISBN: 978-1-4502-3711-6 (ebook)

Printed in the United States of America

iUniverse rev. date: 6/28/2010

Cover photo of Mount Rainier by Michael Baker
Taken Christmas Day 1997
Using a Nikon camera, with a 210 mm lens.
*Mount Rainier has an elevation of 14,000 feet and is located
about 70 miles SE of Seattle, Washington*

To touch the soul
of another human being
is to walk on sacred ground

- Stephen Covey

This book is dedicated to my clients, the brave souls who had the willingness to enter into their inner worlds and the courage to fight the demons hiding there so that they could emerge as the heroes of their inner children. I also dedicate this book to all who are committed to healing on a cellular level. It is through freeing ourselves from the pain our bodies and minds carry that our spirits are set free to guide us in living an abundant life full of joy and true to our purpose. This is the life we were born to lead.

"The first peace, which is most important, is that which comes within the souls of people when they realize their relationship, their oneness with the universe and all its powers."

~ Black Elk

Acknowledgements

∿

"Many hands, hearts, and minds generally contribute to anyone's notable achievements."

~ Walt Disney

I acknowledge the Divine Energy of the God-Source for guiding me on life's journey.

I acknowledge teacher and friend, David Quigley, for bringing Alchemical Hypnotherapy into my life and this world. Learning alchemy from David was a life-changing experience for me and because of knowledge and use of Alchemical Hypnotherapy tI have been able to transform my life, assist others in transforming theirs and write this book.

I lovingly acknowledge my husband Tom for his unconditional love and unwaveringly support.

I acknowledge Hal Zina Bennett, an exceptional and heart-felt writing teacher, whose wisdom and encouragement enabled me to write this book.

I acknowledge James and Rosemary Hughes for opening the doors of crystal healing, scared geometry, cellular and sound healing to me.

I thank Richard Beyer and Terry Cole-Whittaker for their spiritual inspiration.

I acknowledge the many teachers, friends and clients who have taught me so much, please know that you have touched my heart and my life in many enriching and beautiful ways.

Last, but by no means least, I thank iUniverse for the professional publication of this book.

Important Information

The stories in this book are drawn from real situations. Some of them are a composite of several similar stories. The names and identifying characteristics have been changed in keeping with client confidentiality. This differs only where I have received permission, and on occasion, been requested to use the subject's true name. Because many of us share similar issues I have attempted to pick stories that you, the reader, may find helpful.

The information in this book is meant to compliment the advice and guidance of your physician, or other healthcare practitioner and not replace it. If you are under the care of a physician, or therapist, you should always discuss any changes in your regimen with him or her. Because this is a book and not a medical consultation, keep in mind that the information presented here may not apply in your particular case. Whenever a question arises, discuss it with your physician or healthcare professional.

Contents

A word from the Author

When I began writing *Soul Contracts* in 1999 I wanted to share the magic and miracles of this work with the world. Now, eleven years after the first edition was published, I am older, wiser, more confident, and I have also experienced many more miracles through being witness to a greater number of sessions. As a highly creative person, I am easily bored by repetition and Alchemical work is never repetitive or boring. Each client comes; ready to give voice to the inner story s/he has in her/his cellular memory. There is no script to follow, only the guidance of Spirit, and that is something personal for each client and each situation.

For more than three decades I have traveled the path of seeking the highest vibrational work, thought and action that I can bring to clients, students and to myself. After experiencing many different modalities and learning from many teachers, I bring the finest I have to enhance the already powerful Alchemical/Spiritual Hypnotherapy work. There are many wonderful modalities available today, but in my experience, none provides such a complete mix of the conscious awareness, present and past lives, awakening of spirit, and cellular healing as Alchemy.

Although the work I do encompasses far more than soul contracts and past life work, these areas are of great interest to me both because of personal experience as well as the profound healings I have witnessed in others. I write about this in my book *The Bridge Between Worlds: The Miracle of Following the Heart.* One thing I have learned is that no matter where you live, you will meet those with whom you have soul contracts. Providence will move and create the space in time for you to come together, and what is done with such a meeting is up to each one of us. Two things will affect the action taken, as well as the result: the openness of the heart and conscious awareness.

"Ships that pass in the night and speak to each other in passing only a signal shown, and a distant voice in the darkness; So on the ocean of life, we pass and speak to one another, only a look and a voice, then darkness again and a silence."
~ Henry Wadsworth Longfellow

Sincerely and with Blessings,
Linda Baker

Section I
Introduction

*"It takes courage to grow up and turn out
to be who you really are."*

~ E.E. Cummings

Beginning the Work

∾

"Great things are not done by impulse but by a series of small things brought together."
~ Vincent Van Gogh

From a young age I was interested in why people did what they did. At twelve, I remember thinking a lot about the ways that my parents treated me and I began making a list of things I wanted to remember so not to do them with my children, if I had them. I wondered why I felt different from my family, and why many things that were important to them were not important to me and vice versa. These questions led me to become an avid reader of psychology. The study of the mind and emotions fascinated me. At seventeen I left home to become a nursing student, and during my first year at school decided to become a psychiatric nurse. I graduated, married and moved to Seattle where I took the state nursing examination and received my license as a Registered Nurse. My marriage lasted for one year. I didn't realize it at the time, but it was only the vehicle to bring me to Seattle where I could meet Tom, my life partner.

When Tom, and I had our first child we decided that I would be a stay-at-home mom. I continued to volunteer for a mental health clinic and since working with teenagers had become important to me, Tom and I began to foster parent emotionally challenged teens. With one of our first foster children I was presented with the challenge of reparenting - something I knew nothing about. Six months after coming to live with us, the girl whom I will call Beth, spontaneously regressed from her sixteen-year-old personality to that of about age four or five.

Beth suffered from severe low self-esteem. She had been experimenting with various drugs, was a high school dropout and was suicidal. After living with us for a few months she allowed herself to slip back in time and into the emotional state of early childhood. She needed love, support, and a structure that could help her to relearn some basic life beliefs such as, *"I am loveable for who I am," "I am capable,"* and *"My body is good."* I wasn't sure how to help Beth, but I did remember back to a workshop that I attended several years earlier on reparenting schizophrenics. The woman who taught the workshop had written a book. I went out, found it and stayed up all night reading through the pages, searching for the answers to my questions. Although Beth was not schizophrenic, this book did give me confidence and direction in caring for her.

After six intense months of regressive work, Beth grew up and became the emotional age of the teenager she was. This time she had a healthier attitude about herself and her life. She went back to school, received a college degree and lives happily today with her own family.

From this experience I saw how it was possible for unhealthy learned core beliefs to be replaced with new, healthier and supportive ones. I had always believed that the only way to truly heal was to go to the core of the issue and the gift of my relationship with Beth showed me how true this was. Just as a cut with a grain of sand imbedded within it needs the irritant removed to heal, so the psyche needs release from negative thoughts and beliefs to be free and whole.

As I continued searching to find ways that would help myself and, in turn others to heal unhealthy core beliefs, I was introduced to Alchemical Hypnotherapy. This was back in 1985, a time when therapies that encouraged screaming, pounding and re-experiencing one's pain were popular. At that time I believed that one had to experience nearly as much pain in therapy as was suffered during the original traumatic experience in order to heal. To not go into the pain was interpreted as denial or avoidance. I knew nothing about hypnotherapy, and had only heard about hypnosis, which I associated with mind control. I recalled a movie where I saw an elderly gentleman dangle his gold pocket watch in front of a woman's face and say, *"You are getting sleepy,"* and I remembered a stage hypnotist that would make his subjects cluck like chickens. Indeed, I wouldn't have been interested in exploring hypnotherapy at all except that I was given a book by David Quigley entitled *Alchemical Hypnotherapy*. As I read through the pages of this book, I caught a glimpse of how reparenting work could be accomplished in a much shorter time by assisting the client in finding his or her own inner resources. This concept excited me and prompted me to begin studying the healing art of Alchemical Hypnotherapy.

I began this journey by taking a four-day Alchemical Hypnotherapy workshop with David Quigley. On the morning of the second day of the workshop, I awoke to experience a difficulty breathing and felt as if I was being strangled to death. I knew that I needed to find the source of this feeling and quickly! I prayed to know what my body was trying to tell me. The message came through very clearly: *"Leave the hospital. If you stay, it will kill you emotionally and spiritually. You need to follow another path."* At that moment I knew that my only healthy choice was to listen to spirit and deepen my knowledge of this work. I am thankful that I made this choice because Alchemical Hypnotherapy has deeply affected my life as well as the lives of my clients.

When I returned to work, the day after David's workshop, I was again given the message to leave the hospital setting. As I walked through the front door on my way to the adolescent ward I felt a gray air of depression envelop me – a depression that was coming from the staff, not the patients. As I spoke with my co-workers I found that many of them were unhappy and feeling unfulfilled by their work. I also noticed a new patient, a young man of eighteen.

Within moments of walking onto the unit this young man sat down next to me and began talking about how he was certain that something had happened to him when he was a child. He couldn't recall what it was, but he expressed an interest in hypnotherapy as a way of finding out. This was both a surprise and a confirmation of the previous day's message, as no other patient in all of my years at the hospital had ever mentioned hypnotherapy to me. This patient and I had many talks and, although I never mentioned my interest in hypnotherapy, he continued to bring up the subject. As we talked we began to build a trusting relationship and he told me he had checked himself into the hospital because he kept having thoughts of raping girls. He had practiced some acts of sadomasochism on a previous girlfriend and hated himself for it. He was afraid that he would act out more of these thoughts, and believed he had only two choices - one to commit suicide, and the other to ask for help. I knew it was no coincidence that he kept bringing up the subject of hypnotherapy with me, saying, *"I know there is something in my past. I need to find out what it is."*

When the doctor in charge of his case decided to put him on antipsychotic medication, something this young man did not want to take, I stood up against the doctor. This patient was not psychotic, I was certain of that. The day after I resigned from my job the young man signed himself out of the hospital and came home to live with us. He and I worked together using the Alchemical Hypnotherapy techniques I had learned and he did uncover and heal early abuse issues, which included sexual abuse. We both found affirmation in this, him for his innate sense that something in his unconscious was the cause of his problems, and me for the power of this tool. Confirmation came soon after when his sister called, in tears, to tell him that she had just filed a police report against their father for sexual molestation.

When I began practicing hypnotherapy more than twenty-five years ago, I was attached to the *pain + suffering = healing* equation. I always made certain that clients stayed in their pain long enough for me to feel that they were not avoiding or denying anything. The key words here are: *for me to feel*. I now see that the therapist must be completely free of judgment, limitation, or expectation if the client is going to have the opportunity to heal in the fastest and most optimum way.

It was fortunate that despite my own beliefs, the work proved to be very powerful and my clients experienced amazing results. Rather than dealing with symptoms I found that the core of any issue was not only reachable but healable. I saw more profound results with this system than with any of the traditional and alternative therapies I had previously studied and used. With Alchemical Hypnotherapy clients by-passed the symptoms and went directly to the core of their issues. I was excited by the potential of this work and continued training with David Quigley to became certified as an Alchemical Hypnotherapist.

As I write today, I see the consciousness of our planet continuing to grow and expand, and the inner work needed for clearing and moving forward in life has shifted from where it was even a few years ago.

Now I no longer believe that re-experiencing one's pain is a necessity for healing. I have spoken with several people who, although aware that they could use healing, are unwilling, or feel unable to go back and relive the pain of their childhood. Many have been willing to feel their feelings, but have been through the screaming and pounding techniques and are just not interested in doing that over again. Others are not interested in *falling apart* and spending years in therapy, they have lives to live and want to live them. I feel there is wisdom in this. While therapy can help you to feel your feelings and to gain understanding, therapy doesn't need to become your life.

Now I work with energy and through the guidance of the Divine, facilitating a process I call *cellular housecleaning.* In this process, if the client is willing, the cells can open to memory and release information that is no longer serving the individual. After cleansing occurs the cells can be filled with energy that does serve the individuals highest good.

A long and diverse road brings me to my present place of experience and belief. In the pages that follow, I share experiences from my personal life as well as from the lives of clients and friends that I hope will be of service you. Through these stories I hold the intention that you find benefit, understanding and healing in your own life.

I could never have imagined the path that has unfolded before me. I believe that when we are open to new possibilities our consciousness expands, and if we do not become attached to what we do, our work continues to evolve. This is exactly what happened for me. During one session years ago, I began to feel energy pouring out of my hands, and although I wasn't sure what to do with this energy, I vaguely remembered reading something about smoothing auras, so I did that and then an inner voice told me to take Reiki. This was baffling to me, as I didn't consciously know what Reiki was, however, after a period of several months I was led to a healing circle where Reiki was used. I eventually found my teachers and studied this energy system. I have learned to trust my inner voice. That same voice, or higher consciousness has guided me to learn other energy systems as well as bringing the most wonderful teachers into my life. Through listening to inner or higher (whichever you wish to call it by) guidance, I have been led on an incredible journey - every step touched by magic and love.

A Deepening Spiritual Awareness

❦

"Doubt is a pain too lonely to know that faith is his twin brother."
~ Gibran

As I began combining energy work with hypnotherapy my consciousness continued to expand and I was awakened to new possibilities. After about two years of working with the energy, a client who had been terribly abused throughout her childhood and into adolescence came to me. She had gone through many years of therapy with much of it centered on anger release work. At the beginning of our session I encouraged her to move into these angry feelings so that she could express them in the way that I had been taught. She refused. She said that she had yelled, screamed, and punched enough pillows. She was tired of the anger and wanted to do something that would release her from its grip. She wouldn't follow the rules I had learned and I felt at a loss about what I could do.

As she lay there, waiting for me to do something, I remembered that the work I do is guided by spirit and is not about me. I am the open channel that allows Spirit (God/Divine Energy), to do the healing work. With this thought, I turned the session over to Spirit. I let go of my ego's need to find the answer, acknowledged that a power greater than myself held the answer for this woman and said a silent prayer asking that I be a clear vessel for God to work through for her highest good.

I was guided to ask my client if she could become aware of where the anger was being held in her body. She told me it was everywhere. *"What color is it?"* I asked. *"Black,"* she said. *"It's gooey and black and it's everywhere."* I then asked her what she needed to do with this gooey, black anger, and she told me that she needed to let it drain out of her body. *"How can you drain this from your body?"* I asked. She felt and imagined a drain, like a bathtub drain, in the soles of both of her feet. I suggested that she begin to allow this black, gooey stuff to release from each and every cell and move out through these drains at the bottom of her feet.

As she began the process she became more relaxed and peaceful. She imagined this substance going down deep into the core of the earth where it became purified. With my hands held about six inches above her body, I began to do energy work. By this I mean that I imagined the energy from Spirit moving through my hands and assisting her to do the work. I moved my hands gently over her body in a downward motion from her head to her toes. After about ten minutes she said that the process was complete and that none of the old energy was left. I asked that she check each cell with her mind's eye and make certain that it was all clean and clear. After this I asked what she would like to fill this space with. She chose a bright gold light. Together we worked to fill every cell of her body with this light.

After our session, this woman told me that she felt more relaxed, calm and peaceful than she could ever remember. The important thing here is that she was able to anchor these peaceful, calm feelings into her life and continue to bring them into her experience until they became more natural to her than the old feelings of anger.

It is important to replace old, unwanted and unneeded energy with energy that is healthy and supportive, otherwise the old energy will return to fill the space. It is equally important that the client be the one to choose the color and or type of energy to bring in as it is this person's higher self and spirit who knows what is best for them.

This session was a gift for me because it forced me to rethink the paradigm that I had previously believed. Was it really possible for someone to allow the space for true healing to occur without diving into the feelings and sinking into the pain? This client had spent years in therapy where she felt and expressed her pain, but it hadn't brought her the healing she desired. Not only did this process release the anger she held, it moved her into a deep space of peace

and well-being. This presented a very exciting possi   n
this door provided me a more expansive belief abou
could share with others.

I feel that for healing to occur the individual mu.....
give expression to any feeling that arises. If there is judgment about
expressing feelings or judgment about which feelings are *right* or
wrong these judgments {inner critical voice} must be spoken to.
When the critic is quelled it is easier for the energetic system to clear
itself. As I mentioned earlier, Spirit can only assist us in our healing
when we are open and willing. We have free will and if a part of
us is refusing or unable to allow what needs to happen, to happen,
then that part needs to come into alignment with the intention of
healing, for healing to occur. Our state of openness and willingness
is a reflection of how much we are able to love ourselves, and all
aspects of ourselves completely. Sometimes a client who comes from
a religious background or a metaphysical background comes to me
saying that even though their mom/dad/ sister/brother/ uncle abused/
neglected or hurt them, they have completely forgiven them. They
say that through their reading about past lives, karma, forgiveness,
or that we create our reality they understand that it wasn't the other
person's fault or intention to hurt them. But healing doesn't happen
on an intellectual level and forgiveness must go beyond the mind to
permeate every cell of the body.

If the body is in agreement with the spoken word it will show it,
and if it is not it will show that as well. In fact, understanding, when
used to avoid feeling, can even hinder the healing process. Healing
comes from the heart and moves through the body on a cellular level.
Healing comes when every cell lets go of the pain, shame and guilt
to receive truth, love and compassion.

When we try to avoid feelings and carry judgments about
ourselves (like it is not ok to be angry or to speak feelings of revenge,
hate, etc. because it is not nice or spiritual), the ability to love the
self is blocked. The amount of blockage in the body on a cellular
level is a direct reflection of the pain and suffering that we perceive
we have endured, and are still enduring. The more severe the abuse,
the stronger the feelings will be. In this work, expression without
judgment allows the energy to leave the cells. Expression does not

an wallowing in old murky waters or blaming others, it just means being honest. I believe that once it is accepted that the expression of any emotion is in perfect harmony with God and healing, that emotion or energy can be released from the body without going into the drama of the event and sometimes without even having conscious awareness of the trauma.

From countless client sessions I have seen that the willingness to heal allows healing to occur more quickly and easily. Willingness is the key. When clients first come they ask, *"How long will this process take?"* My answer always is that it depends upon their willingness to feel, experience, know, release and receive whatever is needed for their healing. Spirit wants us to let go of old baggage and be who we truly are, but Spirit can only assist us as far as we are willing to be assisted. We have free will. Spirit cannot supersede our will. If we want healing in a certain area of our life but say, *"I don't want to feel pain, or look at my mother/father issues,"* Spirit's hands are tied and we can only be helped in a limited way. It is when we are willing to step out of our own way and fully trust Spirit that the door opens wide and we are fully able to receive all of the gifts that God/ Goddess has for us.

The Process

"At the center of your being you have the answer, you know who you are and you know what you want."

~ Lao-Tzu

The reader may wonder what this Spiritual Hypnosis process is? Is it safe? Could evil spirits come in and take over? Can deceased loved ones really be communicated with? Can one access past lives? And, are past lives even real? I can only attempt to answer these questions from my personal experience, the experiences others have shared with me and through communication with God/Spirit.

I would first like to say a word about hypnosis. There are many different types of inductions that produce trance states. A trance may be light and simply induced by watching a movie. If you have ever experienced emotion while being caught up in a movie, you were probably in a light state of trance. The mind is very suggestible in this state, one of the reasons why TV advertising costs so much and works so well. Trance states can also be so deep that the subject is consciously completely unaware of and cannot recall what they were told while in the trance state. Yet while there is no conscious memory in this deep state, the subconscious mind remembers everything that occurs and will respond to suggestions that are given. These suggestions must be in alignment with the client's value system in order for them to work. For example, if the hypnotist gave his client the suggestion to rob a bank, a law-abiding citizen would not be affected by the suggestion. If, however, the client wanted to rob a bank, the suggestion could support the client into putting that thought into action.

Spiritual Hypnosis work occurs in a medium trance state where the mind and body are relaxed, yet the mind remains consciously aware of everything that occurs in the session. During this process the subconscious mind is alert and aware. The client communicates with the practitioner during the session and remembers what occurred during the session. I take notes during a session because I want the client to reinforce those things that are important and will aid his or her inner transformation

I studied Alchemical Hypnotherapy with David Quigley and was certified as an Alchemical Hypnotherapist in June of 1988. As a student of Alchemical Hypnotherapy, I remembered David telling us that we each needed to find our own strengths and call on our own inner *magic* in order to take the Alchemical process out into the world. David said, *"Don't try to be like me, because I will always be the best David Quigley there is, but go and be the best you there is."* I always remembered this; because this is a mark of a teacher that is spirit-guided, *do not imitate me - be the gift you are.*

Now, through Alchemical Hypnotherapy, spirit was speaking through me and guiding me to find my own special path in this work. As I combined the use of energy, sound, crystals and high vibrational essential oils with Alchemical Hypnotherapy, I felt something was missing from calling myself a hypnotherapist, and began calling myself a *Spiritual Hypnotherapist* so potential clients would understand this was spiritual work. When I teach, I acknowledge that I work only as a guide in the healing process and that all healing and miracles that may occur, come from Spirit. There is a force greater than the personality, ego, and learned techniques at work here. I have no attachment to what label this force is given, because to me it is all One. I use whatever words my client is comfortable with so that s/he feels comfortable and at ease. These words include; Higher Self, Great Spirit, God, Goddess, Universal Energy, Source or Divine Energy and extend to more personal beings as Jesus, Buddha, animal totems, angels and so forth. I want clients to understand that this is not something I am doing *to* them, but rather a way by which they can connect and receive information and healing directly from Spirit.

The process of this work is simple and natural. Take a moment to recall a time in your own life when you felt confused about what to do in a situation, or maybe when you had forgotten someone's name or misplaced an item. If you allow yourself to recall that situation, you might remember that the harder you tried to figure out what to do, to remember the forgotten name, the location of the lost item, etc., the harder it was to remember. You may have felt that your thoughts were *making you crazy* as they circled around in your head. Then, perhaps you forgot about the issue for a time and while driving, taking a shower, or washing dishes, in that moment of relaxed thought, the answer to your problem magically came to you. You may have responded with, *"Now why didn't I think of that sooner!"* or, *"I remember her name!"* or an *"Of course, that's where I left it!"* Where did this information come from? After all, you had searched for it, focused on it, and tried very hard to think of the answer. Why was it that when you stopped thinking, the answer came? Was the answer your own thought? If so, then why didn't you think of it when you were trying? Or, is it possible that this thought came to you from your Higher Self, God, an Angel or a Spirit Guide? The answer is *"Yes."* The yes could be any of these or something else. The point is that when we allow the critical mind to relax we become open to receiving information. This openness and receptivity is the basis of the Spiritual Hypnotherapy process.

If you like, you can experiment by using the following simple technique. Find a space that feels safe and nurturing to you. This must be a quiet place where people, pets, or the telephone will not disturb you. You may either lie down or sit, whichever is most comfortable. It is often best to sit on the floor against a wall or in a chair where your spinal column can be straight and supported. It is important that you have a clear intention for what you would like to do at this time. Your intention could be to connect with a loved one who has died, or to gain insight into a challenge that you are facing in your life. Whatever it is, be as specific as you can about what you would like to do or to know. It could be something like, *"I want to know if you forgive me for not being there when you died,"* or *"I want to know if you are okay where you are,"* or *"I feel like so-and-so and I have had a past connection. I would like to know what that was about."* Or maybe, *"I am so confused about taking or not taking this new job,"* or *"Should I move to Cincinnati?"*

When you are clear with what you want, close your eyes and take in some nice deep breaths. You might try this simple breathing technique: Concentrate on your first breath as you slowly inhale through your nose and then slowly exhale through your mouth. Repeat this process until your mind and body feel calm and quiet. The breath is a powerful tool that can take you deep into that place of healing, wisdom and knowing. Imagine yourself sinking deeper and deeper into a place of relaxation and safety, deeper and deeper into a place of wisdom and knowing. As you imagine yourself safe and relaxed, you can easily begin to count down with each exhale, 10 - 9 - 8 -7- etc. Allow yourself to be as open as possible to whatever images, sounds, colors, smells, or feelings come to your attention. Allow your consciousness to go, without criticism deeper into whatever comes to you and ask for whatever it is that you wish to know. The message can come in any way, in any form. The most important thing is to be open, release control, and be willing to receive whatever comes.

This is a simple outline of the process. Some individuals are able to access past life information or connect with spirit very easily, while for others this process may end in frustration, sleep, or thoughts about what to fix for dinner. Whether or not you are able to access the information you desire on your own is no indication of how spiritually evolved you are. A trained facilitator who can guide you in this inner journey is most valuable because s/he will keep you on course and if an upsetting emotion such as sadness, grief, guilt, or anger surfaces, you will feel the safety of being able to allow the feeling to rise and bring healing. One of the beautiful things about being human is that the love and support we share with each other is so extremely healing. Sometimes we need the support of someone in order to let go and feel our feelings. Sometimes we need someone whom we can trust and who has the skill of working with the inner world to guide us on that journey. This is true for everyone, no matter where they are on their path.

When I facilitate a Spiritual Hypnosis session I do so in a very specific environment. First, I have the client lie on a copper-grid bed surrounded by crystals. This bed makes it easier to connect with Spirit and keeps the client's energy field clear and free of outside contamination. Crystals impart energy of their own and, while they enhance the work and I love working with them, they are not necessary for the Spiritual Hypnotherapy process to work.

During the trance induction I allow myself to go into a light trance as I utilize energy and spiritual work I have learned through Reiki and Reconnection Healing to assist the connection of my energy with the client's and facilitate bringing through the healing energy of Spirit. This connection creates a sense of safety for the client and enables me to be more aware of, and sensitive to his or her process. The trance induction also involves guided imagery, a verbal count down, stating the intention for only the highest good of the client, and progressive relaxation. I also state the intention for communication with Higher Self and spirit guides. Communication with the Higher Self includes a statement about the issue the client is seeking clarification or healing on. This is an invitation to all those in the spirit world who love and desire the highest good for the client to assist with the process. I also include a statement of willingness for the client. This affirms that the client is willing to receive and release whatever may be necessary for this work to be accomplished. I may ask my clients to bring in a white light (or light of any color they wish} and surround themselves with this light. I may ask them to hold the intention that this light keeps them safe, allowing only that which is for their highest good and healing to enter. I hold intention for myself, to be a clear vessel for the session, and for the client to receive what s/he desires.

At the completion of the induction, if I am in physical contact with the client, I remove my hands from the client's body so that my energy does not distract the client from their process. At this time the session becomes interactive and as the client verbally communicates to me, I guide the session by asking questions and supporting the client's process. During the session I work over the body with crystals and my hands and I may use essential oils or facilitate sound or light therapy if that is required. There is no formula for a session as each one is guided by spirit and each person requires different things.

When there is communication with a soul that is not in body, I use my body as an antenna to help facilitate the communication. I sit at the client's head with my right hand about three inches above their forehead, palm down and my left arm, in a comfortable position in front of me, bent at the elbow, with the palm up. When I do this my intention is to be a clear, empty channel so that the energy of the spirit is able to come through and communicate with the client. I began to do this without understanding why. Later a psychic told me that this did assist with spirit communication.

At the conclusion of a session I go over the important events that happened and have the client give thanks to Spirit for this learning. I also give homework to help the client further ground the work of the session in the cells of their body. There is a saying *"Old habits die hard"* and I find conscious attention to the homework for at least thirty days helps cement in the new beliefs. Of course the energy shift has happened and the client keeps the healing energy from the session within the body's cellular memory where it may be accessed as needed or desired.

Authors note: *Alchemical Hypnotherapy* is spiritual work and essentially the same as *Spiritual Hypnotherapy*. Sometimes I use the two terms together.

Section II
The Veil Between Worlds

*"Every person and all of the events of your life,
are there because you have drawn them there.
What you choose to do with them is up to you."*

~ Richard Bach

Recognizing Past Life Connections

~

*"Love is a fruit in season at all times,
and within the reach of every hand."*

~ Mother Teresa

Is love really the answer? It seems to me that it is. When a person is willing to look at a relationship with another, regardless of how painful that relationship may be, there is always love at the core. This may not appear to be the case and we may resist or fight the possibility, but it never the less, it seems to be true. This love may have to do with the present lifetime, or it may be a memory from a past lifetime, a spirit connection, or a combination of all three. Even if we do not remember or want to accept this love, when we are willing and courageous enough to look deep enough, we can always find it.

A strong feeling of love, mistrust, fear, hate, compassion, or other emotion for someone in this present-day life can be explored to see if its roots lie in a present-day situation, a past life, or both. If the feeling makes sense to us in this lifetime because of the relationship we have with the person, then at least part of it has to do with this lifetime. But if the feelings seem incongruent, illogical, or even crazy, then they are most likely rooted in a past life. For example, we may wish to leave an abusive relationship, yet in some peculiar way feel bound to it. We may fear that a certain person will hurt or betray us even though there may be no evidence to support this fear. We may find ourselves with a compulsion to *save* people who do not want or need saving and they may even use our well-meant attempts to care for them as a way to continue their dysfunctional behaviors. There are numerous *could be* scenarios and many possible sources

ا our feelings towards another. They may come from our childhood challenges, reflect aspects of us that need healing; exist as a result of past life experiences, or as a combination of both. The key is to find the core.

So how can we recognize when a past life connection is involved? Look closely at your life. Do you normally find yourself acting logically, but this one relationship seems to make you act in ways that feel unhealthy crazy or out of control and there doesn't seem to be a thing you can do about it? Or do you feel an especially strong connection or attraction to someone for no apparent reason? Perhaps you have experienced an immediate repulsion or distrust for someone that has no logical basis or an unusual familiarity with someone that you've just met. Maybe you've felt like you've known a person before, yet have never met them in this lifetime – a daja vu experience. These are all signs that you could be experiencing a past life soul connection. As you read this book, perhaps some of your own past life connections will become clear to you.

My interest in, and awareness of, soul connections and contracts has come about through my personal life experiences. My study of energy systems, daily prayer, and a willingness to be of service, have opened my awareness to God, and the teachings of my spirit guides and angels who have guided me into this deeper understanding of soul contracts and connections.

Spirit Communication
and Reincarnation

∽

"The real voyage of discovery consists not in seeing new landscape, but in having new eyes."

~ Proust

My beliefs about spirit guides, our own inner wisdom, reincarnation, and our ability to communicate with those who have passed over began when I was a young girl. Although born into a Roman Catholic family, I was never a good Catholic and even as a child, the church's concept of heaven and hell didn't make sense to me. I could not understand how an all forgiving and merciful God could condemn someone to eternal hell with no possibility or opportunity to ever grow or make changes. I remember thinking that I could never condemn anyone to such a sentence, so how could a God who was so much more loving and merciful than me do that? After giving the subject much thought, I came home from school one day and announced to my mother, who was ironing in the kitchen, *"I don't believe in hell."* Her response was, *"Wait until your father gets home!"* My father arrived, and after trying without success to convince me that hell did exist, he drove me to our church so the priest could talk to me. The priest, having no better success than my father, told me, *"You don't believe in hell because you're afraid you're going to go there."* Rather than scaring me into the belief of eternal damnation, his comment only served to discredit him. *"He couldn't come up with anything better than that!"* I thought, *"What a pity."*

During this time I was also questioning the belief that each of us has only one life. I was convinced there must be an explanation for why some people who seemed so good suffered in poverty and illness, while others who seemed cold and uncaring enjoyed health and abundance. Since the church was unable to help me in my quest for answers to these questions I began to think about and explore the possibility of past lives. Doing the best I could to make my thoughts fit into the teachings of my family and church, I finally concluded that the *one life* taught by the church was the one life of our spirit, and spirit could wear many bodies. Little did I know that one day I would discover religions all over the world that believed exactly this.

The more I questioned and searched for answers that made sense to me, the less being Catholic worked in my life and I left the church at age seventeen. At this time I became fascinated by ancient legends telling of gods, goddesses and spirits appearing and communicating with human beings. My attention was also captured by stories that told about appearances of angels and saints within the last century. Information about séances and people who professed to speak with the dead also interested me, but I was afraid to get involved with these things, although I did, gain a reputation for being quite good with the Ouija board.

Though I continued my search, it wasn't until I discovered Alchemical Hypnotherapy in 1985 and received my first past life session, that my belief turned to experience. Even though the session took place many years ago, I can still clearly remember re-experiencing that life in ancient China. I never had been especially interested in China, but during that session the country and the people were as vivid to me as if I had just returned from a visit there.

Interestingly, fourteen years following this session, Spirit directed me to take a specific trip to China, and although I really didn't want to go, the energy of Sprit was too strong to resist. We had fostered several young people over the years and just before leaving on this trip, I told my husband that I didn't want to take in any more problem kids, but I would like to help a young person who just had a bad break in life and would appreciate and use assistance. In China, on a cruise through the Three Gorges on the Yangtze River, I met such a young person. Since that time I have traveled to China sixteen times and it feels like my second home. I helped this young man to go to school and he became my adopted spiritual son. One day while visiting a tiny temple in the midst of the rice paddies by his home, an old monk told him that we had been mother and son in another lifetime. Some years later I wrote the book: *The Bridge Between Worlds: The Miracle of following the Heart* to tell of this powerful and profound adventure.

As I began facilitating sessions with clients, I was presented with increasing evidence that not only were past life memories and communication with the *other side* a reality, but that they were just as real (if not more so) than the physical world. During sessions many clients contacted relations or friends who had just died or who had passed on years earlier. Several things convinced me that these contacts were real. Often clients, came to see me because they were experiencing guilt, grief or stagnation in life as a result of unfinished business with someone who died. After communicating with and receiving forgiveness from the spirit during a session, the client would report feelings of deep love, release and freedom. Often the spirit of the deceased wanted to resolve this conflict as well and we (the client and I) were thanked for making this opportunity available.

Often times during a session, there would be a release of energy that enabled the spirit to move on and go into the Light. On occasion, clients also received information about the deceased person that was not previously known to them. When this information was checked with family members, its accuracy was confirmed. Finally, when a client was communicating with a spirit I would often feel a tingling sensation and experience goose bumps on my arms and legs. Sometimes I would experience a cold wave of energy throughout my body, and sense the presence of someone else in the room. Often my sense of this presence would immediately be followed by either the client's initial connection with the spirit or an important part of the communication. One such session involved a client who came to me for the purpose of exploring his lifelong feelings of abandonment.

Bill, as I will call him, had already experienced several years of traditional therapy. This therapy helped him gain insights into his relationship with his mother, the place where his issues appeared to stem from. He discovered that even after his mother's death he was unable to release her energy and resolve these issues, in fact, since her death these feelings had intensified. Bill needed to reprogram his conscious and subconscious tapes that contained what he learned as a child by his parents and other authority figures because he was still unsuccessfully playing these out of date tapes in response to present day situations.

During a session, Bill connected with the spirit of his mother. Among other things, she told him how unhappy she had been during her pregnancy and how she had attempted to abort him. She felt trapped in an abusive marriage and blamed the baby for her having to stay. Although she eventually left Bill's father and had come to love her son, the scars from this early life experience remained with Bill. This was new information for him. But as insight alone does not heal, Bill scheduled another session. During the session Bill was assisted in creating new pre-birth, birth, and infant memory tapes. In his new memory he was wanted, cherished and loved. During this process he also imagined releasing the old feelings of not being wanted and saw himself, in the present, accepting the love and friendship he wanted so much. After doing this he was able to forgive his mother for how she had treated him and was able to feel compassion for her life. She was thankful for this and told Bill that she had been hanging around him, waiting for him to do this healing. She was now released of her guilt and able to move into the Light. Bill hugged her just before she left. He cried and shared that he felt more tenderness and love from her now than he had ever experienced when she was alive.

After this session, Bill called his aunt and checked out the information he had received with her. She admitted that when his mother learned she was pregnant she was very upset, and had resented the baby throughout her pregnancy and during his early infancy. The aunt said that Bill's mother had confided the abortion attempts to her, but never told anyone else. In fact the aunt said, she went to great lengths to prevent Bill from ever finding this out. This is a profound example of how our feelings affect others, even when we are careful and attempt to hide the truth. Our emotions have a magnetic energy that is stronger than words. And even though an individual may be consciously unaware of these feelings, they still affect him or her on a cellular level. The confirmation Bill received from his aunt was powerfully validating for both he and I. His willingness to open to his emotional pain and pursue his healing process paid off. Today,

26

Bill is a far happier and a more self-confident man who is involved in a loving relationship.

Another example that convinces me that past lives are real is when a client, who has absolutely no belief in reincarnation, spontaneously regresses to a time period of which she or he had no previous conscious knowledge of, and yet can *see* the surroundings with great clarity. With sessions like these, both my clients and myself become aware of how each lifetime is an opportunity to learn specific lessons. These lessons afford us the opportunity for growth and expansion of our consciousness. This explains why some clients, despite their dedication to inner work and therapy, find some issues impossible to resolve until lessons from past lifetimes are fully integrated into their present life. I see this as reclaiming the parts of our soul selves from which we were energetically separated, and bringing them home so that we can be whole. This reclamation offers us expanded energy and a greater ability to live in the present, creating what we truly desire in our lives today.

Working With the Dead

∾

"The last day does not bring extinction to us, but change of place."

~ Cicero

The above quote reminds me of a story I once heard that is a metaphor for death. This is my version of that story:

There was a beautiful sleek wooden sailing ship with snowy white sails sitting in dock at a seaside village. On the day the ship was to set sail the people of the village came to bid her good-bye. As the sails filled with the wind and the ship began to move away from the safe harbor the people stood waving and shouting, some with tears in their eyes, *"Good-bye! Good-bye!"* They stood and watched until she sailed out of sight. But what they did not see as they walked back to their homes, was the other shore. For soon after they said their good-byes the people of another village, in a distant land were shouting, *"Here she comes! Here she comes!"* And like our spirit when it crosses the space between worlds, she is greeted with joy and with love.

I once heard St Francis of Assisi speak through the voice of a channeler. He said that death is like changing our clothes. We watch the newborn child change into a toddler and watch the toddler change into a schoolgirl or boy. We watch as the teenager emerges and then the young adult. We see the transformation into middle age and then the wrinkles and loose skin that come with old age. Death is only the next stage of growth, the only difference is we are not privy to watching the change – not usually, that is.

Part I

"Love cures people – both the ones who give it and the ones who receive it."

~ Karl Mennunger

An aspect of my work that I really enjoy, is communicating with the *dead*. I often say *"I love working with dead people."* I have to be careful whom I say that around, as once I said it to a hospice worker and she asked, *"You already consider them dead?"* That gave me thought as to how to address this subject, as the *dead* are not really dead as it is only the body that loses life. So far *working with the dead* is the best I have come up with.

At one point in my career I considered running an ad saying that I specialized in working with dead grandmothers. This may sound a bit strange, but I had just happened to have four clients in a row that came to clear energy around their grandmothers who had died. I listened to the sadness and guilt that these clients expressed and saw the heavy energy they carried because of words not said or actions not taken. I watched as they connected with the spirits of their dead grandmothers and witnessed the love and comfort these spirits gave to their grieving grandchildren. These clients left my office with a lighter heart that love and self-forgiveness brings.

Then I worked with clients who had children, brothers, sisters and parents who had committed suicide. A grieving mother came because her son had just taken his life and she felt that he had directed her to come to see me. Her session was powerful. Her son shared many things with her and told her that he would be helping her from the other side. After the session she still felt the grief of not having her son in physical body, but her energy was much more peaceful and she was thankful for the information she received from his spirit.

One of the most beautiful sessions I have ever had the honor to participate in was when a young woman came to me because her little sister had committed suicide. My client was pregnant with her third child at the time of her sister's death. The two sisters had always been close and, although she knew her sister suffered from bouts of depression; she had not known how serious it was. My client, whom I will refer to as June, told me how the family had just sat down for their evening meal when the telephone rang. June, three months pregnant at the time, answered the phone. To hear her father's voice on the other end of the line - the shock of his words sent June into a burst of uncontrollable tears. After going through a period of anger, guilt and grief, June became so depressed that she could barely function. She thought about taking anti-depressant medication but a friend suggested that she come and try hypnotherapy first.

After hearing her story, I asked June if she would be willing to connect with the spirit of her sister. She said that she would, but she had fears about doing this. After the initial trance induction, June found herself in a beautiful garden. She felt very young and peaceful. Soon a little girl came to join her. June looked into the eyes of this young girl and recognized her to be her sister Gabrielle. June could immediately feel the love she had in her heart for this young sister. Gabrielle said, *"Do not suffer because of me. See how happy I am here? Do you remember when you and I would pick flowers and make daisy chains? Do you remember how happy we were? This is how I am now. This is how I want you to remember me."* June began to cry as she released the grief that she held around her sister's death.

Then June became angry. I encouraged her to share this with Gabrielle. *"Why did you leave me!"* June shouted. *"You didn't even wait to meet little Anna."* (the child June was carrying at the time). *"Why did you do this when I was pregnant? I've been so worried about how Anna has suffered because of all my depression."* When June finished speaking, I asked her to hear what Gabrielle had to say about this. June, still sobbing, became silent. I noticed her energy shift. The tears stopped and her breathing became regular. She lie still for several minutes and when I asked her what was happening, this is what she said:

Gabrielle says that she is sorry that she had to leave, but she did not know of any other way to end her deep suffering. She said, *"Do not grieve that I did not meet your child. Anna and I met on the spiritual plane. We are kindred spirits. We played together before she came fully into the physical. She is a special child and has not suffered because of your grief. She is a strong spirit and has come to help you,"* With those words, June again began to cry. Through the sobs she told me how she knew this was true. Little Anna had been a solace to her. Whenever she looked into the child's eyes she felt peace.

I instructed June to connect with Gabrielle's energy. As she did this I asked, *"Do you want to hug her?"* *"Yes,"* June replied. I gave June a pillow to represent her sister's physical body. June put her arms around the pillow and embraced Gabrielle. She cried and told Gabrielle how sorry she was that she didn't know how badly she was hurting. June said, *"I am so sorry I failed you! I wasn't there for you! I let you down!"* Gabrielle told June that this was not true. This had been her path to learning and there was nothing June could have done. The sisters forgave each other. I could feel the love in the room as their spirits connected. After the session was over June felt a peace that she had not experienced since her father's phone call two years previous.

I was deeply touched by this session and with the richness of what it offered. I had never before witnessed spirit talking about how souls going from and entering physical bodies can communicate. Several months later I was doing a meditation when I felt Gabrielle's spirit come to me. I asked why she was there, as I did not know her. She told me that our souls did know each other and that she wanted to thank me so much for creating the space for her to connect with June. Again I was moved by the presence of this loving spirit.

Part II

"When you were born you cried and the world rejoiced. Live your life so that when you die the world cries and you rejoice."

~ Cherokee Expression

A young woman named Alice came to me because she had been depressed and felt that her life was not her own. She was always thinking of others and concerned about not hurting anyone to the fault of causing herself suffering. She gave time to others when she really wanted to be alone. She did things for others that she really did not want to do, but she just could not bring herself to say no. Alice wanted to step into her power and stop this self-destructive behavior. She was surprised to find what happened when she reached the bottom of her inner stairway. The following is Alice's account of her session.

"I found myself dancing around a wild bonfire. One of my dancing companions turned out to be my cousin Tracey, who had died of cancer 6 years ago. We never spoke a word, but just seeing her in such health and beauty was all I needed. In this place, she was happy and no longer suffering. Upon realizing that my lack of involvement in her life had no bearing on her cancer or her death, I was able to accept the greatest gift of all; a single kiss on my right check. A kiss from an angel is what I received.

Tracey then left, but came back, hand in hand, with a beautiful, young man. His blond hair and blue eyes told me it was my deceased grandfather. He had committed suicide when I was 10, and from then on, my mental picture of him included him standing with a shotgun by his side. When I saw him in this new place, the weariness was gone from his face and the pain of a troubled life had left him. He was radiant with life, youth and peace. After greeting him, he did the most incredible thing; he pulled out a large shotgun, like I had always imagined him using on himself, and he threw it in the bonfire still blazing by my side. I watched that gun burn, sizzle, and disintegrate into the flames.

Watching that gun burn was an experience I will never forget. My grandfather then asked something of me; he wanted me to travel back, and be with my little brother Ben. Grandpa and my brother were very close, and his passing left deep scars in Ben's little heart. During our first trip back to my grandfather's house after his death, little Ben ran around the house trying to find him – of course, he was no longer sitting in his kitchen chair. At that moment, I, as a 10 year old girl, hugged my 5 year old brother and told him that his grandpa loved him very much, and that his actions in no way were determined by his grandkids. I felt the healing in myself, as well as my brother. It was just as much a moment for me, as it was for Ben.

Later, I shared my experience with my family. They all cried. Ben revealed to me that the only thing he really remembers about Grandpa's death was that mad, failed search for him. He was overcome with emotion when I told him that I held him in that moment, and what Grandpa's message was for him."

This session also helped Alice. She could see how the guilt she had felt about not being there for and not doing enough for her cousins was the root of putting everyone before herself. Maybe, on some level, she was trying to make up for this or punishing herself for not having done the *right* thing. Today Alice is living much more empowered life. Although it has still been uncomfortable for her to say *"No"*, she has been able to do it. The more she honors herself and sets her boundaries with others, the greater enjoyment she is finding in her life. Alice says, *"I no longer envision Tracey dying in her hospital bed, or my grandfather morose with a rifle in his hand. They are dressed in white, young, youthful, and together."* Today Alice is a happy young woman.

Part III

"Joy is a net of love by which you catch souls."

~ Mother Teresa

Samantha was having so much muscle pain in her left hip and leg that she could barely walk. It is interesting to note that the left side is connected to receiving. In the book; *Heal Your Body*, by Louise L. Hay, she says that muscles represent our ability to move in life. Muscle pain represents resistance to new experiences and hip problems, the fear of going forward in major decisions. Samantha felt that the challenge she was facing was somehow related to the recent and unexpected death of a beloved aunt.

During this session, my husband Tom, worked on Samantha's body using crystals, sound and the energetic healing that flowed through his hands. I facilitated the hypnosis session. It was easy for Samantha to connect with her deceased aunt. Her mother and another aunt also made their appearance. Samantha had the sense that part of her issue with this pain was holding on to the past and the fear of letting go meant that in some way she would be letting her family down. This is a common fear that is subconsciously held, especially when there has been both love and abuse involved growing up.

When we love our parents and other family members we want to be connected with them. It does not matter if there was abuse (emotional, physical or spiritual), we still want their love and the connection with them is all we knew as a child. Even people who grow up and hate their families, expressing anger that anyone would even suggest they wanted love from family members, seem to hold this desire and fear of letting go deep inside. Lazaris (a group of entities that channels through Jack Pursel) says that one of the biggest things holding us back from moving forward in life is the fear of letting go of the people we love. If we make a shift and increase our vibrational frequency, and they do not, we will lose the connection with them. On an unconscious level a person may choose to keep themselves in old patterns and sabotage their efforts to change because they are afraid of losing love, or feel guilt in leaving others behind. Since these old patterns have existed for generations and may have been part of our soul's learning for many lifetimes, to let them go now, may feel may

feel like a deep betrayal of the family. This is one rea
pattern feels so safe, and may feel impossible to change

The truth is, we cannot save anyone. All we ca
ourselves and shine our light into the world. In this way we provide
hope and a way for those who seek healing. We can offer them shelter
from the storm, but only if they ask for it. If we keep our vibrational
level lowered and remain in old dysfunctional patterns, we will only
drown with the others. We have the choice to be the beacon or to
hold on to old family patterns – a lifeline that may seem safe, but will
not take us to where our soul longs to go. I have witnessed countless
times as a client made the choice to throw off the old energetic
burdens of family abuse, lack, suffering and addictions, and instead
of feeling betrayed by this, dead ancestors expressed great thanks
and joy because they were freed as well. While in the physical body
a person may have been unconscious to the affects of these patterns
on themselves and others, but now in the spirit world they can see
a higher truth. Often spirits, the ones who both loved and abused,
seem to hang around those they abused, maybe in hope that healing
will happen. I believe that the healing we do in this life runs down a
time-line and brings healing to generations.

I asked Samantha to *"just imagine for a moment"* how it would
feel to release this painful energy. She said, *"I would feel light and
free. The burden would be lifted."* I then asked what her mother
and aunts had to say about this. *"They want me to."* Samantha said.
*"They are party angels and do not want me to wait as long as they
did to lighten up".* *"Will they help you to release this old energy?"*
I asked. *"They already are."* Came the reply. Tom continued to
work energetically over Samantha's body as these dear women, now
in spirit, removed the old burdensome energy from their beloved
child.

It is a beautiful and humbling experience to witness loving spirits
work on a client. I tell clients that I work as a guide for God and Spirit.
It is at times like these when I feel so humble and thankful to do the
work I do and be part of this *Divine Team.* I have witnessed loving
ancestral spirits or Divine God-Source energy work in miraculous
ways as they pull out old, no longer useful energy and release it to
the Light.

I instructed Samantha to breathe into her body and allow them to do the work. It is important to work with spirit and give permission. We have free will and spirit cannot work against it. I also asked Samantha to let me know when the energy was fully released. She answered that some of the energy was connected to a brother. He was an alcoholic and had two young sons whom Samantha dearly loved. She had been trying to get her brother to change and had, unknowingly, allowed his energy into her body. This is commonly done when there is a strong connection (love or hate) between two people, and an accompanying desire to control the person or the situation. The desire is the attachment that connects the energy to the body.

For example: if person A is the one who wants to change the situation and person B is the one who needs *fixing*, Person A, through their desire to change person B, will allow person B's energy to hook up to their own energy system. In this way person A *feeds* person B energy. On some level person A believes that they are responsible for person B and must help them. If they didn't, person A believes that person B would not survive. Wrong! This does not help either person. It drains person A of energy and brings on physical, emotional or spiritual problems while keeping person B stuck in the problem. This belief also discounts Spirit and person B's connection with his/her own Angels and Guides. It is a statement to God saying; *"I know what is better for this person/situation then you do, and s/he is my responsibility, not yours."* This energy attachment works just as easily when there is anger. I have watched this with several clients who were in the process of, or had already gone through divorce.

Several years ago this was expressed beautifully by a young woman who felt her ex was a destructive influence on their children. The angrier she was and the more she tried to shield the children from him, the more he seemed to retaliate. During the session she saw how he was feeding off of her energy. Her attachment to him and what he did allowed for this. When she pulled the plug, she saw his energy whither away. Much to her surprise she saw how she was the powerful one, but allowing him to *feed* on her energy was what made her feel weak and controlled by him. This is a wonderful example of why turning it over to God or Higher Power is *so* essential.

Forgiveness and letting go is not a statement that the other person is right, or that we don't care, but instead it is a powerful, energetic force that allows us to have an open channel with God and be present in our own divine energy.

Samantha understood this and was willing to let the energy from her brother go. She did this with love. A client may wish to keep a stand of golden light between themselves and the other person. This represents love and a Divine connection that is only open to the highest good of both individuals.

When the old energy was completely released I instructed Samantha to call her true energy home (the body is the physical home to our spirit) to fill these places. This is the soul's energy, the energy that serves our highest good. It is the energy that had to leave home in order for the burdensome energy to exist in our cells. Samantha felt the lightness of her energy returning home. Her mother and aunts showered their love upon Samantha and the tears slid down her cheeks as she felt herself fill with their love and care for her. Samantha gave thanks to them for assisting her and for loving her.

Part IV

"Let us love, not in word or speech, but in truth and action."
~ The Bible John 3:18

A friend of mine who recently lost his wife to cancer has two young daughters. He told me that one evening one of the little girls was crying and missing her mommy so much that she could not be comforted. As a student of the Alchemical Hypnotherapy process, he was able to have her imagine going to a safe place where she and mommy could meet. Not only was his daughter able to do this, but she felt comforted by her mommy and was able to *hear* words that her mommy spoke to her.

Is this all imagination? From my experience, I think (and feel) not. My belief is that his daughter's mommy really did visit and comfort her. Often when we are close to someone, especially when there is a need, as a child has for a parent, spirit chooses to stay close by.

My friend now does an Alchemical/Spiritual process with his daughters whenever they need or want to talk with mommy. Spirit can communicate with us when we are open and this process allows us to still the mind, open the heart and become aware so that we are able to connect with those who live in the spirit world. It appears that the more we are aware of and are willing to communicate with spirit, the thinner the veil between the physical and non-physical worlds becomes. Not only can we in the physical body receive helpful information from the spiritual realm, we can reciprocate and offer this healing opportunity to spirit.

Several years ago, a student of mine was able to connect with a young nephew who had died at fourteen years of age. We were doing some work in that place where spirit dwells when this boy came up and contacted him. The boy, needing help to move through some pain, had been waiting for his beloved uncle to die and move into the spirit realm where he could help him. Now, with this process, he was able to receive what he needed and was free to move into the Light without his uncle having to die. During the session the boy said, *"I am so happy that you are doing this! Now I can move on!"* Many, many times in doing this work, spirit expresses deep gratitude for the client's willingness to enter into this space, communicate and do healing work.

One morning, my husband Tom awoke to tell me of an unusual dream he had. It was one of those dreams in which you can't tell if you are awake or dreaming. He was lying on our bed when he heard someone out on the balcony. He could see the shape through the curtains and so he asked, *"Who's there?"* It happened to be a young man (I will call him Edward) whom we had foster-parented several years ago. Although he had done much good work, was away at college, and seemed to be doing his best ever, Edward had committed suicide. In this *dream* Tom felt he came to ask for help because someone was after him. Even while relating it next morning, Tom felt upset by this *dream*. He felt that Edward's soul was calling to him.

I was surprised to hear this because I had my own experience of Edward's spirit visiting me shortly after his suicide. On night he visited me he was laughing, his energy was bright and a glowing silvery light surrounded him. He said, *"Mum, mum* (as he called me) *I just came back to tell you how happy I am! I can't stay. I have to go now."* I noticed great beings, possibly angels behind him, and then they all left. I felt joy and peace in my heart. Because of this experience, I wondered why Tom had this experience.

I asked Tom if he wanted to receive a session so that he could communicate with Edward, and he said that he would. As we began the session, Tom entered into a space where he felt Edward's energy. Edward told him that he wanted our forgiveness for some things he had done while living with us, and said that he loved us. Tom replied that we had forgiven him and that we loved him as well. At this time, Tom felt a strong, energy vibrating through his hands and extending throughout his entire body. Tom said, *"Edward's energy is very powerful."*

I asked if Edward was willing to share with us why he had taken his life. He was willing. He told Tom that he had been doing poorly in school, but that this was not his reason. He had been spending more and more time out in the wilderness and was feeling very connected with Spirit. He shared that his drop in grades was a reflection of the fact that his spirit was already leaving. He said that he made the decision to take what he had learned and then return in service for healing on the planet. He said that he left with this intention and it was not related to fear.

Near the end of the session, Tom sensed a cord was wrapped around his own heart. He was told that this had been present for protection, but now that time was over and the heart needed to be freed if Tom's energy was to flow completely through his body. When Tom said that he was open to this, a spirit guide came in and released the cord. Tom sensed the energy flowing through him and his heart felt more open than ever before. Edward seemed pleased with this occurrence and began to fade away. It appeared that he had come to Tom to help him. We both felt this was his gift to Tom for all Tom had done for him.

When I related this story to a friend, she commented that when Edward spoke of returning to serve the planet, he might not have meant returning in a physical body, but rather working to serve through the spirit realm. My body tingled when she said that, so it feels true to me. Edward's gentle nature certainly lends itself to that possibility.

The question I am sometimes asked is *"Is this fact or fiction?"* Again, from personal experience and from sharing this work with others, I have no doubt that soul connections and our ability to connect with spirit are real. Often when a spirit enters the space where a client and I are working, my body responds with chills and goose bumps and my hair stands on end. Sometimes I am filled with an almost overwhelming sense of love, like during the time when a man with many difficulties connected with his loving grandmother. This man had been to many therapists and felt little hope in what I could do for him. The spirit of his grandmother came in the room and began lifting layers of fear and depression off of him. He was bathed in her love and it was this love, not my doing something, that helped him. Clients often respond in a similar manner when spirit connects with them. They may feel icy cold, which often is a sign of spirit, or they may experience deep, sometimes overwhelming emotion or a strong feeling or sense that a person is with them in spirit form. This, plus the fact that information imparted by spirit has often been found to be true, gives me full confidence that the spirit world is very near and within the reach of conscious communication. With this work the client directly experiences communication with spirit instead of having a third party interpret for them.

Part V

"Emotion always has its roots in the unconscious
and manifests itself in the body."
~ Irene Claremont de Castillejo

I've become accustomed to the spirits showing up at sessions to help with the work and I am frequently moved to tears by the tender help they extend toward those they loved and left behind on the physical plain. I always hold prayer that those who I can benefit will come and find me, but sometime a client comes, and while telling his or her story, I think, *"Why have they come to me? What can I do?"* In that moment I am reminded that it is not me, but Spirit working through me, that does the work.

Such a story was Jeffery who came because his mother wanted him to. Jeffery was in his mid-thirties and suffered from agoraphobia (fear of open or public spaces) so severely that he was refusing to leave the house. After my telephone conversation with Jeffery's mother, she felt that this spiritual work could benefit her son, and so she got him out of his apartment and drove him to see me.

During our interview Jeffery expressed uneasiness about being in the healing room and told me that he didn't think this would help him, but that he was doing it for his mom. As he went on about listing all the therapists, psychologists and psychiatrists that could not help him, I had that thought, *"Why is he coming to me? If they couldn't help him, what am I supposed to do?* Again the *voice* reminded me that I was a guide and it was God/Divine Power and not me who did the work.

At one point during the session, Jeffery felt the energy of someone familiar. It turned out to be his grandmother, a woman whom Jeffery had loved dearly and who's passing was very difficult for him. Grandmother told Jeffery that he had many fears and memories of the past buried inside of him and she would like to help him let them go, if he would let her. Jeffery agreed, as he had great trust in her; and so the process began.

It was amazing to *watch* Jeffery's grandmother work on him (watch is italicized because I was not watching in the conventional sense, but sensing this happening on an etheric level, through the third eye of sight). It felt like a surgical procedure as she cleaned out the old energy. Jeffery lay there, breathing, receiving and allowing the experience to unfold, while I provided additional energy work to assist the process. Upon completion, I asked Jeffery to breathe into his body and invite his spirit in to fill these spaces. I asked if there was a color to the incoming energy, and there was, gold. As he filled himself with this golden light, he became lighter and felt better. I had him future pace, go forward in time to see how his life might be a little different. He did and he saw himself, at ease and happy, walking in the garden and visiting friends, two things he had not done for a long time.

Then I used another technique and asked him to imagine this new self, six months, one year, and even five years from now. *"How do you look and how are you feeling five years from now?"* I asked him. He said that he was standing tall and that he felt so good and connected with life. I then asked him to look into the eyes of that one of him, five years in the future, and ask if he had any advice for the Jeffery lying here on the table – he did. He told Jeffery, just keep in touch with this golden light and remember you are safe; just do what you are doing and you will be here. I then picked up a brass Tibetan bowl that I often use in healing work and told Jeffery that I was going to make a sound over his body and wanted him to breathe into it. As the bowl vibrated with sound I told Jeffery, *"The past is the past and the past is over, today, right now you are stepping into your new life."* I had him imagine that one of him five years in the future standing there, as the Jeffery of now walked towards him. A session like this is humbling for me because it is a miracle, and to assist and be present for such healing is a gift I deeply cherish.

The Story of Byron

❦

"Love is the greatest power there is."

~ Patricia Sun

I am convinced, through my personal work and work with others, that it is the intention and thoughts we hold at the time of death that imbed themselves in our very cells and come back with us when we return to a physical body. I used to think that the best way to leave this body would be to die peacefully in my bed. From my experiences with Spiritual Hypnotherapy work I have come to know that it doesn't matter if we die peacefully or traumatically, what matters is where our energy is when we make that shift into spirit. If we die with fear, resentment, anger, guilt or shame, we carry this turmoil into our next incarnation. If we take the feelings of peace, forgiveness and self-love to our death, we incarnate with that peace even if the body experienced a traumatic death.

It is good to know that a soul who has left in confusion, guilt, or sorrow can be reached after death, and healing can occur. Through this work, it is as easy to connect with someone who died a long time ago as it is to connect with someone who has recently made the transition. I hold the vision that there will come a time when each of us who passes will have someone who is willing and able to connect with us. Our friend will make certain that we are all right and are where we need to be. The following story of my client Marie and her nephew Byron is a wonderful illustration of this work.

Marie came to see me for a session shortly after her nineteen-year-old nephew, Byron, was killed in an automobile accident. Byron had been attending college and doing all of the *right* things. He was popular, smart, and his future looked bright until the unexpected ıead-on collision happened. Naturally his whole family went into shock with this unexpected death. Marie had done spirit work with me before and wanted to see if she could gain some understanding of this tragedy. Her first statement to me was, *"I know that he's alright. He's spirit. It's the rest of us that need help."*

My response was that Byron might be all right, but not necessarily. Often when a soul is taken so abruptly, without time to prepare for death, there is confusion. The soul may not even realize that the body is dead. I suggested that Marie might wish to locate Byron by going into a trance state and entering that place where spirit lives. She was very willing to do this. As she let go and allowed her body and mind to relax, she became aware of Byron. The following is a partial transcription of the session.

"I don't understand what you're doing, but it's very cool!" said Byron when she found him. He had been killed instantly in the collision. Moments before the accident he was driving his truck along a sunny Arizona highway, then suddenly he was looking down upon his broken body and his grief-stricken family. He was scared, confused, and didn't know what to do.

"What can I do for you?" Marie asked. *"I just want my body back!"* was the reply. *"This wasn't supposed to happen! I like that body!"* Byron had been close to his mom and was crying because he had never wanted to cause her such pain. Marie witnessed his suffering and asked for others who had gone before to come and comfort him. A great silent, peaceful presence came and surrounded him. Next his great grandmother, whom he had never met in the physical world, came. Such a gentle spirit she was. She took Byron's hand and told him that he needed to trust. He wanted to trust her so much. He could feel her love for him. Next, a man, who Marie did not recognize, came in and identified himself as Sally's dad. Marie did not know who Sally was. He said that he had loved Byron dearly and now was here to comfort him. Finally, a young man appeared who said, *"This place isn't bad once you get used to it. You'll like it here."*

Byron began to relax and as he began to feel the caring energy of these spirits he was able to realize that he had passed through the thin veil that separates the physical realm from the spirit realm. As he began to fill with light, his fear dissipated and he realized that his family was suffering so much partly because they sensed how terrified he was. Now that he was feeling safe and loved he knew that, on some level, they would sense this and it would help their grief.

Byron gave messages to Marie for his mother and his father. He also told Marie to tell his grandfather that he wished he could just give him one more hug. At this time he realized that spirits could visit in dreams, so he added, *"Tell grandpa that whenever he feels hugged in his dreams to know that it's me. Tell grandma that, too."* His girlfriend had broken up with him just weeks before. He sent her the message that this was not about her and added, *"This is an old cliché, but it is true: It is better to have loved and lost than never to have loved at all. Thank you for giving me the opportunity to have experienced love in this way. I love you and I always will."* He told his parents that he was happy they were having his body cremated and the ashes scattered at a place called Hidden Lake. Then he was finished. He said that he would be sending them light and love from where he was. He was feeling the excitement of being in this new home with these souls who loved him. He waved goodbye, and Marie watched him disappear into the Light.

You might ask, *"But how do you know this is real? Maybe her mind made this up so she could feel better."* I can answer that question through these examples: Marie did not know Byron's parents had decided to have the body cremated, nor did she know about this particular lake. After the session Marie called Byron's mother and found that these were the exact plans that his parents had made. Marie had no knowledge of who Sally or Sally's dad were. When she asked her sister about this she was told that Sally was her sister's best friend. Sally's dad was a very close family friend who loved Byron like his own grandson. He had died three years prior. It is also interesting that after the session Byron appeared to three family members. These *visitations* were positive experiences. Marie flew to Phoenix for the funeral. When she shared this information. It brought peace and healing to family members and friends. While sharing the experience Marie realized that the *silent, peaceful presence* that came through was the presence of God.

What about the statement, *"This wasn't supposed to happen?"* As I was writing about this incident, it came to me that Byron's spirit had agreed to this assignment before coming into the physical plane. During the session it was clear that both his parents and others would gain peace and strength from having to experience this loss in their lives. When Marie returned from the funeral she told me how it didn't make sense to her that Byron was surprised by his death. She said that he had talked to some friends the morning of his death and told them, *"If I don't see you on Saturday night go and visit my parents, they will need to talk to you."* To his sister's best friend he said, *"Take care of her, she's going to really need a sister,"* and in a card that he wrote that day, celebrating his mother's birthday, he wrote, *"I hope that I will be here to give you a card next year."* This was crossed out and followed by, *"Why did I write that? Of course I'll be here."* From these incidents I can only suspect that the spirit was aware of the agreement but the nineteen-year-old personality did not remember it.

This story shows us how even the death of someone we love can be a gift for our own awakening. It appears that Byron could have made a contract with members of his family to assist them in their growth and understanding through his departure. The more experience I have with Spirit the less separation I see between the two worlds.

Exploring Soul Connections

⁓

"Only when the clamor of the outside world is silenced will you be able to hear the deeper vibration. Listen carefully."
~ Sarah Ban Breathnach

If you are interested in exploring past life soul connections, or connecting with the spirits of those who have passed on, I highly recommend working with a hypnotherapist trained in Alchemical Hypnotherapy. Without a guide you may find your mind wandering or relaxing into sleep. An experienced guide can gently help keep you on focus and enter into where your cellular memories are stored. There may be some fear associated with retrieving past life memories, and that is normal. This fear may have its roots in the anticipation of remembering personal trauma or a time when you may have been the perpetrator. A knowledgeable guide helps to create the safety necessary to enter into healing, and can provide you with valuable insight. Also, an experienced guide will assist you with completing communication, bringing healing into the situation, and releasing cellular energy that no longer serves you.

Your guide may direct you to do a body scan to either verify a clear energy field or locate any remaining energy that needs to be cleared. While in the trance state it is easy to imagine looking at or feeling each cell of your body. You are easily able to move from the top of the head down to the tips of the toes and notice any energy cords that do not belong. You can then release these cords that bind you to others and clear yourself of any contaminated energy. Once these places are clear you can invite any parts of yourself that moved out of your body to come back home and fill these spaces. This process nables you to reclaim your personal power, live in wholeness, and gain access to all of your energy. Often, a client will feel an actual physical shift in the body when the lost part or parts are called home. A vibrational and emotional shift is also common. You may wish to have this information recorded, either written or taped, so that you can refer back to the spiritual guidance you received. For more on this subject please refer to the chapter on forgiveness.

Connecting with a departed soul on your own may be easier than attempting past life healing. One way to do this is to take a picture of the departed (if you have one), a letter, or anything that either belonged to or reminds you of this person, and put it on a table by your bed. Set your intention that tonight you desire to communicate with this one. You may use the exercise in Section One, The Process, of this book as you lie in bed, only this time, as you count down, imagine yourself going to a special place where your souls can connect. This might be a favorite spot where you used to meet, a special dream temple, or anywhere that feels right to you. Though you may fall asleep, your intention and openness may enable the spirit to connect with your consciousness through the dream state. Before beginning this journey, set your intention to remember the dream and have a pen and paper by your bedside so that you can record key points of the dream as soon as you awake, even if this is in the middle of the night. It is best to record the information as soon as possible because even a very vivid, *"I'll always remember this!"* dream can be easily lost. Also, just having the paper and pen available gives your subconscious mind and Spirit the message that you truly desire to make this connection. Doing this is good for remembering any dreams.

I have used this technique successfully myself. About two months after a dear friend died, he came to me in a dream that was like no other dream I have ever had. It was a very clear and physical experience. We sat together and I could hold him in the same way that I can hold a living body. It was a powerful and loving experience. He told me that he had to move on and do the things that he had to do. He said that he had come to say goodbye in this way so that we could be together this one last time before he left. I will always remember that experience. It was several months later when I read that these special, physical dreams are one of the ways in which spirit is able to communicate with us.

Section III
Contracts Between Souls

*"Your friends will know you better
in the first minute you meet
than your acquaintances will know you
in a thousand years."*

~ Richard Bach

Introduction

∾

"We can do no great things, only small things with great love."
~ Mother Teresa

Often we hear about soul mates. Many people read about, take workshops on, and go searching for their soul mate or twin flame with great zeal. They are driven by the idea that a certain person will fulfill all of their desires. Maybe this is true, maybe not, either way this is not what I am talking about when I speak of soul connections.

Soul connections can show up in many different forms and may cover a broad age range. My belief is that when our hearts are open to allowing soul connections into our lives they occur naturally. *Coincidence* unites souls who have contracted to come together in this lifetime. It appears that souls come together to help each other evolve. This is why some of the strongest soul connections can carry us into our deepest places of pain and fear and into our deepest places of love and transformation.

We have the free will to recognize the energy of a soul connection and learn from it, or to deny the experience and move away from it. Those with whom we have these connections and contracts may be in our lives for extended periods of time, or they may pass briefly by. It is not the time, but the lesson that is important.

Sometimes there is a soul connection and a contract that is made at birth or in early childhood, as with one young, obese woman whom I worked with. As soon as she would begin to drop excess pounds, she would put them right back on. We found that she had a contract with her mother. She was her mother's friend, and one of the things they did for fun was to shop – in the *large women's* department. If she lost weight she would betray her contract with her mother. Or like the young man who was charismatic, bright and a hard worker, yet still could not succeed. He made a contract with himself after his parent's divorce. His mother repeatedly told him how hard she worked for so little so he contracted that he would never do better or have life easier than she did. He perceived that with this bond she would not leave him, like his father did.

The question often asked is *"How can I recognize a soul connection?"* In the pages that follow I will share with you stories of soul connections. Some are from my personal experience and some from my work with others. As you read them, some may feel familiar to you, and may remind you, in some ways, of relationships in your own life or in the lives of people you have known. In these pages you will find clues for recognizing soul connections and contracts in your own life.

Michael

"Where there is great love there are always miracles."
-Willa Cather

I first became consciously aware of the soul connection phenomenon when I met Michael. Michael had just been diagnosed with AIDS and was, understandably feeling quite depressed. A mutual friend of ours referred him to me for hypnotherapy work and when he sat down for our initial session, the first thing he said was; *"You work with guides, don't you?"* I answered, *"Yes,"* and asked him how he knew. He told me that he saw them, and went on to describe the three guides he saw standing behind me. He was surprised that I didn't see them.

As he lay on the mat before me, I saw a sheet of black energy covering him, and so I knew that his situation was serious. The session was gentle and I began to feel a deep sense of caring for this man who lay before me. We scheduled a second session for the following week. When the day of our session arrived, Michael was too ill to come to see me, so I went to him instead. This time I gave him a Reiki session. Reiki is a form of hands-on healing that allows the practitioner to channel the energy of Spirit through to the client for the healing of mind, body, and spirit. On the day following the Reiki session Michael called to inform me that he had been admitted into the hospital with a serious case of pneumosistis pneumonia.

It just so happened that I was face painting at a laughter and play conference the day after Michael's hospitalization, so at the end of the conference I gathered up a large bouquet of stray balloons, bought a pint of chocolate Hagen-Daz ice cream (Michael's favorite), and entered the hospital complete with a brightly painted clown face. Michael was delighted!

After he returned home, I visited him several times a week. I gave him more Reiki energy as we talked, shared our lives and just enjoyed being together. Soon Michael was faced with the difficult decision of staying in Seattle or moving back to Arizona with his parents. He wanted to do some relationship healing work with his father and so made the decision to move.

I knew that I would go and visit Michael. However, that visit came sooner than I had expected. When I called Michael one Saturday morning a few weeks after his move I could hear the shakiness in his voice over the telephone, and although he always did his best to be positive, this time the quiver in his voice gave way to tears. He related how his stepmother had thrown the classified ad section of the newspaper at him that morning and told him to find another place to live. Michael suspected that she feared that having a son living with AIDS at home would be bad for her career. The day before, when her colleagues came to the house for a business meeting, she instructed Michael to stay in his room. While her behavior hurt Michael, what devastated him the most was the passive agreement of his father.

Michael soon moved into a tiny cottage where, almost immediately, he became very ill and had to be hospitalized. Since being in the hospital was not Michael's favorite place, and since I was a nurse, his doctor agreed to send him home if I came to care for him. As I flew to meet my friend I wondered about this situation. Here I was, a married woman with two children at home, flying down to take care of a man whom I had only known for two months. It seemed a bit strange and I couldn't explain it, yet I knew it was the right thing for me to do, and fortunately my husband respects and supports my need to follow my heart and the voice of spirit.

The week before traveling to Arizona I had taken a medical hypnosis class that provided me with more tools that I could possibly use to help my friend. Filled with optimism that I could *save* Michael, I arrived to find a different story in place. Michael had resumed smoking and was not interested in any of what I had to offer, including the Reiki that he had previously loved to receive.

I'll always remember that first night as I lay on a
the floor just outside his bedroom door breathing in ci;
and feeling angry that he didn't want anything to do w
came ready to give. In the middle of my poor me, angry· ..ιui-nim fit,
the *Voice* spoke and said, *"If you can't be with him in the way that he
needs you, then leave."* There was something about the quality of that
voice that brought me back to center and made it clear that I had to
make a decision. If I wanted to be with my friend then I needed to let
go of my expectations and be with him in the way that *he* needed, and
if I couldn't let go of my needs, then I had better get on the next plane
and fly home. I made the decision to let go and to stay. For years I
had been praying to deepen my ability to love without condition, and
here I had the perfect opportunity to practice. I cooked for Michael,
sang to him and cared for him. We sat on his bed watching hours of
old movies, talking, laughing, and crying together. I felt so blessed
and so loved by God. I felt great joy and was thankful to have this
special time with my dear friend.

Michael's mother and grandfather visited often. His grandfather
was great! He would take us to the hospital for Michael's appointments
and after I left he was a wonderful support to Michael. Leaving
Michael after these two very special weeks was difficult, but I knew
that I would return. I was unsure of how I would afford to buy another
plane ticket so soon, but I needn't have worried as Spirit took care of
that for me. The day after returning home a client gifted me with two
round-trip tickets. That gift made it clear that I was supposed to be
with Michael again soon and I went to see him three weeks later.

The day after returning home from my second visit with Michael
his mother called and said he had suddenly gotten worse and was
back in the hospital. At the time I was leading a healing circle for
people with AIDS and I had to wait for nearly a week before I could
leave. Each time I called Michael's mom, or his doctor, they would
tell me, *"He's waiting for you to come."* His mom told me that he
asked daily, *"Is Linda here?"* She would say, *"No, two more days."*
He would then turn over and go back to sleep.

During our last visit together Michael had made it clear that he
wanted to die at home and had asked if I would stay with him. When
I arrived at the hospital he sat up, as best he could, and tried getting

out of bed, but his body, frail and blue from kaposi's sarcoma, would not co-operate. Though he wanted to go home his family and doctors would not let him leave and sadly, I knew that decision was best.

I spent the next fourteen hours with my dear friend. Most of the time we were alone while I talked to him, sang, and stroked his face and hands. I could feel the presence of his grandmother's spirit in the room. She had died a few years earlier. Michael had been very close to her and had told me many stories about her and now I knew she had come to help him make the journey to the other side. I felt grateful for her presence.

One of my favorite sayings is: *"If you can't find humor in something, you're taking it too seriously."* Even in this situation I had to laugh because whenever the nursing shift would change, the new staff would stop by Michael's room to say hello to me or to offer to get me something to eat or drink. Being a nurse myself, I could only imagine how in their staff meeting they talked about how this patient's friend had flown here from Washington to care for him. They treated me as if I was a saint and I chuckled inside to imagine how surprised they'd be to find I had only known Michael for such a short time and that I was following something that I didn't even understand.

I finally went on a short break to Michael's mother's house. I started out on a much-needed walk, when after only a few steps I heard, *"Go back."* I didn't want to. I was enjoying this time outside in the warm night air, and I stubbornly walked on, but the voice persisted and so, reluctantly I turned back toward the house. As I entered, the phone rang with news that Michael was ready to leave. His mother and I got in the car and drove to the hospital.

We arrived to find several family members gathered at his bedside. The nurses had Michael's bed cranked to full upright position because he was having so much trouble breathing and I went to stand next to him, stroking his face and kissing his cheek. I told him to just let go. It was time to go. As I stood there feeling the love I had for Michael, I noticed a sheet of white light over his pelvic area. My eyes followed that light all the way up and out the top of his head, where it expanded, then disappeared. As I watched it leave Michael's body, I was filled with utter joy and ecstasy! I had never witnessed spirit

leaving before, and I felt such tremendous joy! When I
at the body I felt nothing. It could have been a wooden
there in the bed. It was obvious to me that Michael, m
was no longer there and his spirit had left it's earthly home.

I learned an important lesson from Michael's death. Even though
I had been enveloped by great joy at his spirit's leaving, for many
days following his death I could not even think of my friend without
sobbing as though my heart would break. I never thought I would be
able to say his name again without the tears erupting. I remember
going to the florist with his mother and grandfather to choose flowers
for the funeral. In memory of Michael's love for the Hawaiian
Islands, I chose a beautiful bouquet of Hawaiian flowers. It took me
by surprise when the woman at the counter gave me a card and told
me to write a message on it. What do you write to a dead friend? As
I thought of what I would like to say to Michael, I lost control and
began weeping so hard that I had to sit down at the desk. Michael's
embarrassed relatives quickly departed the shop, saying they would
meet me in the car.

During this time, it helped me to remember the words of Francis
of Assisi as channeled by a friend. Francis said that it is important to
allow ourselves to completely feel our feelings. He said that if we do
not allow full expression of ourselves, we keep the feelings locked
within our cells. Francis advised that whether our feelings are: grief
or joy, we need to feel them completely and let them go. I allowed
myself to follow this wisdom and experienced how, even with the
joy my spirit felt, my physical body needed to grieve the loss of not
having my friend with me on the physical plane.

Until my experience with Michael's death I had little curiosity
about past life and soul connections. Now, because of the intensity
of this experience, I decided to explore these ideas through Spiritual
Hypnosis. I found that Michael and I had been together for many
lifetimes; in fact I was surprised to find that our soul essence went
back to the beginning of time. I learned that in this lifetime Michael
needed to experience being a gay man and I needed to experience a
marriage with children. Michael had known that his transition from
this lifetime was going to be difficult and, because of the love we
shared, I had contracted to be with him at his time of death.

To some this may seem like pure fantasy, but it is my truth. Michael and I had grown up on opposite sides of the country. I had moved to Washington and he to Hawaii. Although Michael passionately loved Hawaii and was successful in many endeavors there, when spirit spoke to him, he listened. He was told to sell everything and move back to the mainland. He had a friend in Colorado whom he decided to go into business with, and though that partnership did not work, it did lead to a relationship with a man named Bill who *just happened* to come from a town near my home in Washington. Michael and Bill decided to move back to this town and shortly thereafter Michael became sick and was diagnosed with AIDS. Although he had never gone to a therapist, when a mutual friend recommended that Michael see me, he did.

From this experience, I believe that when a contract is made, the souls will come together regardless of geographic circumstances. We don't need to search for our soul mates or other soul connections; they will find us. No matter what the time or space, souls who are meant to meet will meet, all we need to do is to hold our heart open and be willing to recognize the connection when it comes. Of course, events will unfold as needed regardless of whether or not we recognize the contracts involved, however, recognizing soul connections can lead to greater understanding and deeper healing.

After Michael's physical death, I could feel the presence of his spirit around me for several weeks. The most memorable event during that time occurred when I was called to a hospital to do Reiki on a man, whom I will call John. John had AIDS, and was so delirious that even the medications prescribed by the doctor could not calm him. As I walked into the hospital that night I asked for Michael's help. When I arrived, I saw John's partner and several of his friends anxiously watching John. I walked to the head of the bed and pushed it away from the wall so I could put my hands on his head in first Reiki position. Incredibly, as soon as I did this, John relaxed completely and the room became silent as everyone looked at me in awe. I couldn't tell them that Michael was there with me, assisting souls who were stuck to John to let go and move into the Light. Within minutes, John was sleeping soundly.

As I left the room, John's partner followed me out. He thanked me for coming and then told me that John had been leading an AIDS support group in which several of the members had recently died. When I heard this, it made perfect sense to me that these souls were clinging to him. Sometimes if a person is afraid to die, their soul might cling to someone to whom they feel connected, and in this case, that person was John. When this happens the soul needs reassurance that moving on is not only safe, but also desirable. Michael's part was to help these souls to realize this so that they could cross over into the Light. From my own work with people living with HIV/AIDS, I know that sometimes there is fear that when they die they will go to hell, and so there was no better spirit than Michael to help them move on. I believe that these souls were draining John's already fragile energy system and when they were removed John's energy went back to supporting his body.

Although this was a powerful experience for me, I was not prepared for what happened the following day when I stopped by to check on John. When I entered his room I found him sitting up in bed. He looked right at me and said, *"Thank you for being here last night."* That shook me. The only time I had ever seen John was the night before when his eyes were closed, and he was thrashing in his bed. Except for the brief moment it took me to walk to his bedside, I was behind him until he fell asleep. So, how did he recognize me? I can only believe that he saw me through his spirit eyes. John recovered quickly and returned home. He continued to lead his support group for several more weeks and died peacefully at home about four months later.

Michael came to me in a very vivid dream a few weeks following our visit to the hospital. He came to tell me that he had other things that he had to do and that he would not be as close by me as he had been. This dream was so real, and I thoroughly enjoyed this last moment with my dear friend.

I am thankful for the all the gifts Michael shared with me, especially the awareness of soul contracts and connections. A wonderful example of this awareness recently came into my life when a friend told me the story of a client who was just married. She and her husband met on an airplane. He had noticed her in the airport and she noticed him noticing her, and it just *happened*, that by *coincidence* they were assigned seats next to each other. It also is true that, even though they both now live in Seattle they were both born in, Newport, Rhode Island where their families still reside. They happened to be back East visiting at the same time - Coincidence? I don't think so. My guess is that they have a soul connection.

Marc

"Life is a pure flame and we live by an invisible sun"
~ Sir Thomas Browne

Several years ago my daughter Vicki asked if Tom and I would be willing to consider becoming foster parents for a boy whom I will call Marc. Marc was in Vicki's class and had to leave his family because he could not agree with their religious beliefs. He had no place to live and was frightened. We had not taken someone in for about six months and were thinking that it was time to stop foster parenting and let our biological family have a year alone together. Our daughter would be leaving home soon and our time remaining seemed precious and short. I also had a hypnotherapy practice in Seattle and, knowing how much time a new foster child requires, felt that it would be too much for me to take on. We did agree that he could come to a summer party at our home and so we met. Although he seemed like a nice young man, I had no desire for him to live with us, but the Universe did, and as we were talking on the stairs in our home, a curious thing happened.

At the precise moment I was going to tell Marc the decision was *"No,"* a friend of his, who had briefly dated our daughter, walked in, uninvited. My previous experiences with him had left me feeling that he was an energy vampire (a term for someone who sucks other peoples energy from them) and could not be trusted. I knew that he had offered Marc a room in his apartment, and the thought of Marc moving into that situation didn't feel good. Just as this uninvited guest entered our home, I saw the room fade into blackness, and at precisely the same moment I felt like someone reached in, grabbed my intestines, and began squeezing them until I yelled, *"Okay, I'll take him! Just let go!"* This all happened in a moment within my own consciousness and I was left stunned by the experience. The pain immediately stopped, and I knew Marc was supposed to live with us. There had been other times when I had known a young person was to live with us, but none as dramatic as this.

Marc and I had a strong connection from the beginning. We talked about spirit and energy easily and openly, even though he had not previously discussed these concepts with anyone. As our relationship developed into one of caring and trust, many significant moments occurred, yet three incidents in particular stand out as excellent soul-connection examples.

One night Marc and I were talking in his room. He was propped up on pillows, back to the headboard, and I was sitting crossed-legged at the foot of his bed. The light in the room was dim and we were having a comfortable conversation, when, all of a sudden Marc said, *"I see you as an old man with a beard!"* A few moments passed and he said, *"Now I see you as an old woman!"* From teaching past life regression classes I recognized the exercise of looking into someone's eyes until you can see into their soul and recognize a past life personality. While I had used this exercise in class many times, personally I had never seen someone's face change form.

As I looked across at Marc and as I listened to him talk about how he was experiencing my face changing form, this phenomenon took place for me as well. All of a sudden I was looking into the face of a beautiful young black man, and it scared me. It scared me so much that I closed my eyes. Then I asked my spirit, *"Let me see this one more time."* I opened my eyes, and for an instant I saw the image once again before it vanished. I felt a bit shaken by the experience and I didn't understand its meaning. I told Marc what I had seen and he asked, *"If I was beautiful, why were you scared?"* Thoughts of black magic and sorcerers raced through my mind but nothing made sense, so I only said, *"I don't know."* And I didn't. I was perplexed and I found it interesting that Marc, a white boy who felt such a strong connection with the black culture, came to me in a vision as a black man.

The second event happened when Marc told me that he was planning to sign up for the army. Desert Storm was in progress and he thought he would like to join the armed forces and go to war. I have always encouraged my children to pursue their ideas for life and have been quite open to them making their own decisions, but my response to Marc's statement surprised me. I became angry and desperately tried to talk him out of joining the army. I was demeaning about his interest in the military and found myself saying anything I could think of to stop him from making that decision. We argued about it and although I could not understand the intensity of my reaction, it was there.

I asked my spirit for guidance in this situation, and the perfect opportunity arose. A student from my hypnotherapy class needed to give a session before she could complete the past life part of the program and so we agreed that she would give me the session. As I sank deep within, I found myself, a black woman, in a small wooden boat floating down the river. Very soon I came to my village and my son, whom I recognized as Marc, came running up to meet me - I knew it was he from the eyes. (The eyes are the mirrors to the soul and during past life regression you can recognize people from your present life through the eyes.) It was a joyous reunion! He was about seven or eight years old at the time. We lived in a very loving and peaceful village. A man, who was my friend Michael in this present life, (the same person in the last story) surprised me by showing up. I believe that he was Marc's father, or maybe a chief at that time. (You will see my reason for thinking this in just a moment.)

Time passed and Marc was about sixteen years old. It was time for a ritual ceremony where he would be taken into the tribe as a warrior. He and I were in a small straw hut together and he stood while I kneeled in front of him, fastening a beaded belt around his waist. It had what looked like a piece of red horsehair hanging from the center

In the next scene, our village had been attacked and my present time physical body, the one lying on the mat in front of the student, began to shake as I began a deep, uncontrollable sobbing. I could not finish the session. I knew something horrible had happened and I could not bear to look at it. This was very unusual for me, because by this time, I had received numerous sessions and had never before been unable to come to completion no matter how painful the session might have been. I knew that I would have to return to that place to complete the lifetime and about two weeks later I had the opportunity to do just that.

In another hypnotherapy session I returned to the past life scene after the attack. I found myself walking through the jungle desperately looking for my son. I finally found him, strung up by ropes, quartered and hung in the trees, a terrible thing to see. Now I understood why such fear came up when I saw that beautiful black man as we talked that night, my cells were beginning to recall this memory and, because of the intensity of the trauma, a part of me did not want to remember. It also made sense why I reacted so angrily when Marc talked about joining the military.

There was one more incident that revealed more about our connection. Some weeks prior to my session, Marc had been depressed and was experiencing a difficult time, and nothing I could say or do helped to ease his pain. I went, as I often do, for a walk down by the lake to be alone and to pray. Two years ago, just before his death, my friend Michael had showed me a very old beaded necklace with red horsehair hanging from the center, he collected antiques and told me how this had belonged to a warrior. Although I had no interest in the piece, he carefully took it out of its box and showed it to me on three different occasions. Because of the importance it seemed to hold for him, I took it with me after he died. I put it away and never thought about it until Marc came to live with us. I repeatedly had the feeling that I should give it to him, but I shrugged it off. I didn't think that a seventeen-year-old boy would be interested in this rather bedraggled beaded necklace, but that day as I walked by the lake, I actually *heard* Michael's voice say, *"Give him the necklace!"* I went home, retrieved the piece from its little box, and took it to Marc. I started out with, *"I don't know why, but I'm supposed to give you this."* Explanations weren't necessary as his immediate and powerful emotions took over; he loved it! His reaction surprised me because at the time I had no understanding as to why Marc would feel this way. After my session, however, it made perfect sense. This necklace I had given him was amazingly similar to the belt I had fastened around Marc's waist in that past life. My guess is that there was a matching necklace that I did not notice. Could this even have been the same one? It will always be an unanswered mystery.

After completing that past life in the second session, I told Marc about my experience. We both had tears in our eyes and he said, *"It is like I came back to you at the age I left that time so we could complete our relationship."* This statement was very moving and I could see how the contract had been made for us to complete this past life's drama in our present life.

This true story shows how past life soul connections, memories and contracts can affect our present-day relationships. It is easy to see how, if left unresolved, these connections can cause illogical and even hurtful reactions. The connection could even destroy a relationship through fear and control rather than strengthening it with love and understanding.

Peter

"Those who cannot forgive others break the bridge over which they themselves must pass."

~ Confucius

During our time as a foster parents, I connected with a young man whom I shall call Peter. From the first time we met, both Peter and I felt a sense of recognition; in fact, he thought that he had met me before in his home state of Minnesota. Because of my previous exploration into soul connections, I suspected that one existed between us.

Peter was very troubled; abandoned by his biological parents when he was a small boy, spending time in several foster homes and having a drug addict father who was constantly in jail. As time went on Peter increased his involvement in the drug culture. He lied, did not come home when he said he would, and could not be trusted. Since I had done a lot of inner healing work and foster care before this relationship, I was surprised with how difficult the situation was for me. I became depressed and could do very little in my own life. I felt completely co-dependant and crazy as I found myself centering my life on trying to help Peter. I felt drained of energy and no matter what my family or friends said, or how I felt in my *sane* moments, I couldn't break this energy cord.

At one point I became so drained of energy that even going out to dig in my garden, something that usually brings me joy and energy, was no use. Things got so bad that one day while cleaning, I bent over and felt a sharp pain in my back that resulted in a herniated disc. Thankfully I studied energy enough to know that this was the result of giving so much of my energy away. That was a big wake-up call!

And so I decided to call a woman who does psychic readings. Her phone rang, she answered and asked me to call back in ten minutes as her husband needed to make a call. I waited and called. *"Honey!"* she exclaimed, *"What is going on with you? All this dark energy came right out of the phone when you called and I had to cleanse my house."* I told her how I was feeling and she told me that I was being psychically attacked. As soon as she spoke those words my energy shifted and I felt a lightness that I hadn't felt for days. I felt like my old self. I told her that I didn't believe in psychic attacks, she laughed, and I will always remember her words. *"Do you believe that energy can be sent for healing?"* I replied, *"Yes, of course I do."* She continued, *"Then why don't you think it can be sent to bring harm? Honey, with what you are doing it is dangerous for you not to know this!"* I realized the wisdom of her words, energy is connected to intention, and intention can be either for the positive or the negative. She told me this energy was being sent to me by one of Peter's friends, someone who didn't want me trying to get him off drugs. I learned two things from that phone call. One was that if I choose to be connected with someone of low vibrational energy, they are probably hanging out with people of similar energy and being in this energetic field would affect me. The second was to be aware of my energy and if I noticed a feeling of depression or low energy to stop and check to see if it was my own or coming from someone else. This is easy to do, just ask Spirit/God, *"Is this mine or does it belong to someone else? If it is mine let me know what it is about and if it belongs to someone else, let it be gone."* This has worked well for me and many times when I have used it I have sensed the shift happen and felt my energy restored. We are always in control of what energies we accept into ourselves, we only have to be aware.

Finally I received a hypnotherapy session that helped me detach from Peter's energy. During the session, I imagined talking with Peter, and when the hypnotherapist suggested I look above his body and connect with his higher self, I felt a surge of energy that made me feel as if I had been plugged into an electrical socket run through every cell in my body. Peter's Higher Self spoke to me saying, *"This is the energy that you remember. It is not his body or his behavior that you are connected with: it is this energy. You came down here other to learn, but he is not willing to be responsible for , at this time.*" Right there I got it. It was as if someone had woken me up from a dream and I fully realized that the connection we had while also realizing that I did not have to participate in the abuse or see myself as a victim to his behavior. Seeing the greater picture gave me understanding and helped me to sever the energy cord between us and separate from him. I was now felt free to move forward in my life.

During this session, a movie played out before me and I was shown how each one of us decides what lessons and experiences we want to encounter in order to grow. We make our alliances with others in the spirit world that are willing to help us achieve our goals, and then we incarnate into the physical, dress up in costumes known as bodies, and begin the play (or drama). We forget we are wearing costumes and that we chose our life lessons. Until we remember this, we believe the illusion and perceive that events are happening *to* us instead of *for* us. We often perceive others are causing our pain and feel victimized by them, instead of realizing that they are in our life to provide us with opportunity to grow and expand our consciousness.

From this experience with Peter, I now understood why some people who want so much to get out of an abusive relationship are not able to, even when they see how destructive it is to their lives or their children's lives. The contracts that bind us together in a past life can be even stronger then those of this current lifetime. We can remember the energy of a soul and feel our love and connection to it, but it does not mean that particular soul has embodied with the intention of following a path compatible with our own, and it is not our responsibility to try and make it so.

Despite the shift in energy around my situation with Peter, I began having some feelings of guilt about separating my energy from his, so I decided to explore this further in another session. In this second session, I was the mother of two children. Our family was very poor and my husband ordered that I should sell one of the children as a servant. I had no choice but to do his bidding and so sold the eldest, whom I recognized to be Peter. As I saw these events unfold, I received that Peter had been carrying around the issue of

abandonment for many lifetimes, and this was the issue [...]
chose to heal in this lifetime. I also was told that it was ir[...]
we heal this abandonment issue together because one c. ___
for this lifetime was self-love. At death in that past life I made the
contract that, if given another chance to have him as my son, I would
never abandon Peter. I believe this was why I allowed myself to be
abused and could not simply walk away from the situation.

Through Alchemical Hypnotherapy I learned that although the
spirit connection between Peter and I was beautiful, it had nothing
to do with present life choices or behaviors. I saw that my first and
foremost lesson in this was to love myself and honor my life. I was
now able to make the choice to do this because I released the guilt
that would not allow me to let him go. I was now able to honor his life
and his choices, regardless of how I felt about them or what I thought
would be best for him. I learned that it is my responsibility to trust
that God is in charge, and I do not need to know or understand why
the other person is choosing to walk a certain path. I need only be
accountable for my life and my choices.

This view may sound self-centered because we are so often told
to *do for others*, but we must examine *why* we are doing for others.
When we express compassion, caring, and assistance to others from
a place of clear intention that is not attached to creating the outcome
we want, we exhibit unconditional love. The only life that we have
the right to control is our own. It doesn't matter how many right, good
or loving reasons we create to fool ourselves into believing that we
know what is best for someone else, we are not in charge anyone else's
life or destiny. When we attempt to change someone else's situation
we only prolong the lesson for them as well as for ourselves. When
we send our energy out to change someone else's life, we lose the
energy that we need to live our own lives. It is important to watch for
signs of this behavior, which we are all prone to. These signs include
depression, anxiety, physical ailments, and lack of energy.

I once heard Carolyn Myss tell a story about a woman who prayed
vigilantly for many years fort her brother to stop drinking. Finally,
one day during her prayers, an Angel spoke to her and said, *"You've
been praying wrong."* Angered by this, the woman asked, *"What do
you mean, wrong?"* The Angel told her to simply send prayers of love

and acceptance (unconditional love) to her brother. A few days later her brother called to say he entered an alcohol treatment program. I ask; *"Whose lesson was this?"* Did the brother continue his drinking so his sister could gain this gift? What part do our attachments and well-meaning prayers and advice play in another's life? If she had gotten the message earlier, would he have given up alcohol earlier as well? This is certainly worth reflecting on

I received a reading from a friend during this difficult time. He told me: *"You must let him go with love or Peter* (energetic situation he represented) *will return to you with a different face."* I knew the truth of his words. If we do not let go with love and forgiveness we will attract the same lessons over and over again. I prayed and finally came to a place where I could see the bigger picture. I knew Peter came into my life to teach me about loving and honoring myself. I gave thanks for all I had learned from this experience and also knew that by letting him go in love, I was not abandoning him, but giving him the freedom to make his choices. I still felt love for his spirit, and by disconnecting from his energy I was taking care of my inner child and loving myself. The most valuable lesson I learned was that I need to love myself first, as each one of us does. You are the number one person in your life. This is why it is written in the Bible; *"Love your neighbor as yourself."* When you love you, you will gain the freedom to fully live our life as well as be able to share a pure and healthy love with others. My back healed completely without medical intervention and for the past ten years I have enjoyed a whole new quality of life and relationships. Though grateful for all I learned and gained from this past relationship, I am very clear that I never intend to repeat it again!

Kate & John

❧

"Every person, all of the events of your life are there because you have drawn them there. What you choose to do with them is up to you."

~ Richard Bach

One of the joys of doing this work is the knowing that Spirit is always present and guiding the process. The more open one is, the easier it is to *hear* the *voice* of spirit. When doing and teaching this work, miracles often occur and I would like to share one particularly memorable miracle with you here. I was teaching a hypnotherapy class entitled *Etheric Plane Communication*. During this lesson students learn powerful tools that enable communication with anyone, dead or alive. This communication allows understanding and healing to take place between the client and whoever is being communicated with. Normally, we give one session demonstration on Sunday. But, when we walked into class on Saturday one of our students, Kate, expressed that she was having severe back pain. Instead of beginning class in the usual way, I asked the class if they would like to see how Etheric Plane communication works in dialogue with the body. Everyone responded with an enthusiastic *yes* and so the session with Kate began.

During the session, Kate shared that when she entered into the center of the pain in her back, she found her brother John. She wasn't very happy about finding his energy there, yet she knew that when one commits to healing and is open to the process, it is often the situations and people we don't want to look at that show up. These are the ones who are the *pain in the neck*, back, head, etc. More accurately, they are the ones who we have our energy attached to.

Kate's process was a fairly quiet one, with much of the work being done internally. Those of us in the room could only guess at what was happening as she lie in front of us experiencing her feelings, which turned out to be of hurt, anger and betrayal directed towards her brother John. Finally, Kate came to a place where she was able to begin the process of compassion and forgiveness for John. As her body began to relax and she started to release the anger she had held, it became clear how not being able to forgive her brother John was disabling her own life and keeping her from living from her center. Kate became acutely aware of how deeply this lack of forgiveness was affecting her life and the way she moved through the world.

During this experience of releasing angry, victim energy, Kate was able to bring in the soft, sweet energy of forgiveness. She was able to breathe this energy into every cell of her body, and as she did so she could feel a shift occurring. When she opened her eyes and returned to her full waking consciousness, the back pain had not disappeared but it was markedly less. Kate had not chosen to disclose revealing facts during her session, so neither the other students nor myself was aware of what her situation with John was.

The miracle of this event lays not so much in the session itself, but in what followed. On the third day following this inner dialogue with her brother, Kate received a letter from him. This is significant because they had not communicated for at least ten years. It is also noteworthy that he began the letter on the very day she signed up for the hypnotherapy class, but did not mail it until the day she had received the session.

Kate later pointed out to me how, in his letter, the only thing John had asked her for was forgiveness. He had been praying for this for a long time. Kate feels that his prayers and thoughts helped open the space for this session and the healing that followed. She felt that his intention for healing helped guide her spirit to taking these classes and I agree with her on this. Through this work I have become aware of how we are connected energetically, especially to those we love, and how that connection can and does affect us.

During the next weekend of our class, Kate shared her brother's letter with me. Students were paired up for an exercise, so I had time to read he letter. As I began to open the envelope I received a strong message to go outside and read it in a quiet space. I stepped out and sat on the stairs in front of the classroom. As I held the paper in my hands I felt the words touch my soul. (An excerpt from the letter appears below.) I sat crying as I felt the pain written into these pages, as well as the pain of others who have been on both sides of this victim/perpetrator cycle. I was so moved that I asked Kate if she and her brother might allow me to share their story in this book. They both agreed and it is their hope, as well as my own, that this soul connection work will be an asset in ending the perpetrator/ victim cycle of others as well as help bring understanding and the possibility of healing to pedophilia, a condition that our society considers contemptible and untreatable. And so, they share this excerpt from John's letter with you.

> *"The reason that I'm writing this letter to you is to say how sorry I am for sexually molesting you when you were younger. There is no excuse for what I did to you. I never should have touched you in a sexual manner in any way, shape, or form at any time. I want to express to you my deepest level of guilt, remorse, and how truly sorry I am for what I did. I've got a sickness called pedophilia, which is a disease in which I get sexual pleasure from children.*

> *I've had this disease for many years. I want to express my deepest regret for any emotional trauma that you've suffered in the past and for any emotional trauma that you still are suffering to this day. Nothing that happened back then or now is/was your fault in any way, shape or form. Brothers aren't supposed to do these kinds of things to their little, helpless sisters.*

> *I'm now in a group for sexual offenders and I have been for most of the time since I came to prison. It's*

part of my therapy. I've talked to them about writing this letter to you. They made me realize that because of the suffering that I've caused you to go through all these years that you might not want anything to do with me, that there's just too much pain and suffering that I have caused you to go through. I truly hope and pray this is not the case, but if it is I'll accept your feelings. I dearly miss the special closeness that the two of us used to have, the late night talks and the car rides we used to take to the dock by Chism Park. You have always been special to me.

I hope this letter will start some communication between us about the effects my actions have had on your life. It is hard for me to fully understand and comprehend how my actions have caused suffering in people that I've known. I can only guess what this has done to your life in the sense that I was myself molested by a classmate when I was ten years old. I'm just beginning to understand how this has affected me ever since. I can only imagine it much worse for you to have had it be your own brother as the one who molested you, someone who you are supposed to be able to look up to. Someone who's supposed to look out for and protect you and love you. Lastly I ask if it is possible that sometimes in the future that I can have your forgiveness.

I know that you can never forget what I did to you when I molested you. If there's anything I can do for you, please let me know.

Love, your brother John

Kate shared that if she had received this letter before we had done the session her response would have been *"Fuck you!"* and the letter would have been thrown into the garbage without ever being opened. Because of the deep healing that she was able to do, and her willingness to enter into true forgiveness, she was not only able to read the letter, but was moved by it.

Shortly after the letter's arrival, Kate and John's mother passed away. John was briefly allowed out of prison to attend the funeral. Kate had not seen her brother for over ten years and now he stood in front of her, locked in iron shackles. Here, beside their mother's coffin they were able to able to embrace each other and Kate was able to share her forgiveness with John.

I asked Kate if she would be willing to do another session with me to see what past life connections and learning might be a part of the larger picture of this story. She was willing to do this. When we later met for the session, Kate was feeling resistance to finding what this connection might be, but she proceeded with the session.

In the first part of our session, Kate was taken into a field where members of her tribe were chasing her. She was a Native American man. When we went back in time to find out more about this situation she found that she was a healer, a shaman. The chief's wife and child were in serious danger from childbirth and the chief had called her to save them. As she held the baby in her hands she knew there was nothing that she could do. The child died and the angry chief ordered that she be killed. The chief from this lifetime was her brother today. Kate went to her death in that past lifetime feeling betrayed and angry. She made the decision that she would not use her *magic* again. In that place between lives where spirit lives, Kate saw that the lesson from this lifetime was to accept her gifts and accept destiny.

In the next lifetime Kate was a young man of seventeen. Her brother from this lifetime was also her brother then. He was nineteen. There was a lot of competition between the boys, and out of anger Kate stabbed her brother in the heart and killed him. The awakening of her cells to this memory was intensely emotional. As she felt the knife sink into his heart, she heard his last words, *"I'll get you, you bastard!"*

Kate was cast out of the family and left to wander for the remainder of her life. She died, frozen to death, alone in the wilderness. As Kate remembered those events, she could physically feel her hands and feet becoming cold and numb as the freezing occurred. She remembered that her final thought was to never be alone again. At this point in the session, Kate went into that place in between lives, and received a message from her spirit guides. The message was: *"You cannot hold hate in your heart. Hate will kill you and your spirit. All of our lessons serve us. You must forgive."*

As Kate began to fill the cells of her body with the golden light of forgiveness for herself and for her brother, she began to experience healing, wholeness, and freedom in her body. When we checked in to see if this energy work was completed Kate saw how she and her brother had brought their parents much pain in that lifetime. The guilt from that life was still held in her body's cellular memory. In the session, she was able to release that energy, and as she did she began to feel the grace of self-forgiveness for that situation enter into her cells, replacing the guilt that had been held there. At this point, I was doing energy work over Kate's body and received a very strong message about self-forgiveness.

Often I have heard others say and have even said myself, *"It's so much easier to forgive someone else rather than myself."* The message in this is twofold. First, I do not believe that we can truly forgive another without forgiving ourselves. Second, it is so much easier to forgive someone else because of the fear we have of self-forgiveness. If we truly forgive ourselves then we *have* to forgive others. This means we must release the victim role. This means we have to step into the full power of who we are. The message that Kate received in her past life regression, *"You cannot hold hate in your heart. Hate will kill you and your spirit. You must forgive,"* is a very powerful statement. When she heard this, Kate said, *"I gathered back my energies as I forgave first my brother, then myself."* Forgiveness of her brother was freeing, but self-forgiveness was the most powerful and healing aspect of the equation. Forgiveness of herself was essential for Kate to feel self-love.

This story again shows how we take the emotions and thoughts that we die with into the cells of our next physical incarnation. We can either choose to act them out again in the present incarnation or choose to become conscious and reach forgiveness, understanding, and compassion for others and ourselves. If we take the unconscious route and act out our hate and revenge, we continue on the karmic wheel of suffering. To me, this is what hell is. We create hell for ourselves, not God. Through our hate and unwillingness to forgive we do a marvelous job of condemning ourselves. Through forgiveness, we restore health and well-being, reclaim happiness, and find our inner peace.

The Importance of forgiveness

∼

"Forgiveness is the final form of love."
~ Reinhold Niebuhr

The story of Kate and John shows us the great importance of forgiveness. Holding on to resentment, anger, guilt, or any emotion connected to our lack of forgiveness towards others or ourselves only serves to hurt us on both the physical and energetic planes. Many issues of lack, such as lack of health, money, success, loving relationship, happiness, and energy may be associated with a lack of forgiveness.

But how do we truly forgive on a cellular level? I'm not talking about *New Age* magical thinking here, but true cellular release. So many times clients have come in with a story that includes some version of, *"My mother was an alcoholic and beat me, but I know that I chose her as my mother to learn a lesson. She was abused as a child and did the best that she could with her children so I forgive her."* The clenched hand, subtle tightness of the jaw and stuck energy belie the words. Even though the desire to forgive may be there, until the cells of the body are released of their pain and toxicity, the words are just a sham that attempts to make the person appear to be nice.

My belief is that forgiveness can only come when we are willing to allow the cells of our body to open to our feelings, no matter how painful the feelings might be. With this opening we have to be willing to love ourselves enough to allow all of the emotions to come forth, true and free of censorship. These may include some not nice feelings and words. There may be feelings of hate and anger accompanied by thoughts of punishing, mutilating, or even killing those whom we feel have harmed us. Whatever comes up must be allowed expression for true healing to happen. The expression of such feelings may take time or may last for only an instant, but they are toxic to our body, mind and spirit and must be released. We may not even have conscious awareness of the incidents behind our feelings. The release, understanding and forgiveness that come is completed safely in our inner world with the help of our guides and higher self. No harm is done to anyone on the physical plane. By going through this door we enable the stuck emotions to be released from our cellular structure, and thus set others and ourselves free.

Many times I have had clients who are afraid that if they express their truth, it will in fact harm the other person. This is opposite from the truth. It is the holding on to old energy that causes harm others as well as ourselves and it is when we release this energy that we create space for healing and compassion. For example, imagine you are angry with your father, yet each time he calls, you try to be pleasant. When you pick up the phone and first hear his voice, you may feel your stomach tighten and your energy contract. Your body is expressing the truth of how you feel, and so even if your words are nice, the energy you feel extends out to your father and on some level he feels your anger. He may speak angrily or defensively toward you in response to the energy he feels, and not your words.. This gives you more reason to justify your anger and stay in your victim role. You can tell your friends about how nice you were and how mean he was to you. Your friends may be sympathetic towards you because you seem so nice, and you may never choose to take responsibility for the energy that you put out to him, which is the same energy that is eating you away inside.

When you clear anger and pain from your body by expressing your truth, and genuinely forgive your father, as well as yourself, you take back your power. Now when you pick up the phone and hear his voice, your energy is clear and the possibility for him to behave differently is created. Your new energy may allow him to relax and come off his defensive guard. This clearing and forgiving is healing for both you and him, and it all can happen on the Etheric Plane.

Through Alchemical/Spiritual Hypnotherapy we can communicate with someone else in a clear and honest way on an energetic level.

When this happens we connect with the other person's truth in a way that is healing and forgiving. For example, during Etheric Plane communication, you may find that your father treated you so harshly because he loved you and felt that this is what he needed to do for you to turn out all right. Maybe this is what he learned from his father. In the state of hypnosis you can feel your hurt and anger, scream at your father and do whatever you need to do to make sure that he knows how his treatment of you has affected your life. When the anger is fully released you can share with him how you wanted him to be there for you, how you missed him and how much you love him. This complete sharing of <u>all</u> the emotions allows for true forgiveness and healing. Communicating in this way on the Etheric Plane is often far more powerful than if we attempted to do it in the physical. Because we can express ourselves in whatever way we need, the energy that binds the other person to us can be cleared and we become self-empowered.

We always do this work for our own healing, but when we clear our energy and empower ourselves the side benefit is that we also release the other person. This frees their energy to make other choices. They may choose to move closer to or further away from us, to love us more or become angry because we no longer are willing to have the same dysfunctional relationship with them. We may choose to share our experience of healing and forgiveness with the person involved, if they are receptive, and we don't have to. It is good to know that this process can be complete without ever directly involving the other person.

If you have feelings of anger or resentment when I speak of release and healing for the perpetrator as well as the client, you may want to look at your own belief of being a victim. Etheric Plane communication takes us beyond the victim/perpetrator cycle and shows us the big picture where healing for everyone is a delightful and freeing experience.

How do feelings and thoughts get stuck in our cells? My belief is that the anger we hold in our cells is in direct proportion to the experiences that created it. What comes forth from us is only a reflection of the abusive experiences that has taken our power and stolen pieces of our soul. By abuse I am talking about that which

has frightened us, hurt us and kept us from being our ʌ
self. When we can let go of judgment for what is *ac*
unacceptable for a *good, spiritual,* or *nice* person to fʻ
ourselves the blessing of honesty. Once our cells release tl   .ʌ.ıɑ
in our bodies, they can begin to bring in a new energy of healing,
grace, and forgiveness. Any parts of us that had to leave can be called
back, and returned so that we become whole. In shamanism this is
referred to as soul retrieval.

I've begun to imagine that our bodies are like jigsaw puzzles. You
might remember a time in your life when you were putting a puzzle
together and tried to make a wrong piece fit. You might have felt tired
and frustrated that you couldn't find the right piece, and so you really
wanted it to fit. You may have thought, *"It looks like it should fit,"*
and maybe you could have jammed it in so it looked lie it almost fit,
but if you left it there it would have thrown off the whole puzzle and
distorted the picture. That's how it is for us. Instead of being born
with our unique puzzle intact we may have incarnated with some of
our pieces already missing. They may be stuck in past life beliefs
and dramas that we are not even aware of. In place of our authentic
puzzle pieces we may have squeezed in pieces that did not fit. These
misfit pieces may have been there for so long that we believe they
are our true selves. We may have continued to give away more of our
true pieces during our present-day physical incarnation, beginning as
early as the time of conception. For each piece that we gave away we
might have stuffed in other pieces from parents, teachers, or others
whom we have tried to please. These misfit pieces may be made up
of wanting to be seen as good, or of trying to please, but they are
always made of our desire to avoid pain. Of course, these pieces never
fit quite right.

Why would someone give pieces of themselves away? The answer
is simple: for survival. For example, I had a client notice that instead
of her own *puzzle piece,* her mother's energy was living in the center
of her body. Her parents had divorced when she was a young girl,
and her father left the family. She was very scared that her mother
would also leave and so she sent away her puzzle pieces that had to
do with independence and success. She tried to make her mother's
low self-esteem and fear of failure fit into that part of her. She did this

because she was afraid that if she were independent and successful she would lose her mother's love. Her mother might become jealous or angry and leave her just as her father had.

We originally put these misfit pieces in place to protect ourselves. But why do we become so attached to these feelings that aren't truly ours, even when they don't feel right? I believe we do this because they are often all we remember feeling. We may have taken on these feelings early in life, in the womb or brought them forward from a past lifetime. We falsely believe that they are who we are, and so the thought of releasing them is scary because we fear that we will lose ourselves. The truth is, we will reclaim our power and our true selves.

Because of the unconscious and cellular nature of such decisions they may be difficult to realize and to locate. Spiritual Hypnotherapy helps the client find the places in the body where another's energy lives, release that energy, and reclaim the piece that was given away. With the client I just mentioned, we released the piece that was her mother's and she called back the piece that was hers. Her piece had to do with personal power and success. She no longer needed to protect her little child-self by keeping her energy subdued because she had lost the fear of her mother's anger. Upon calling this piece back she immediately felt a sensation of completeness in her body. Bringing these authentic pieces home brings greater wholeness and healing into our lives.

How long does this process take? It can take one session or several. The amount of energy it takes depends upon the abuse suffered, how strong our attachment to victim energy is, and how willing we are to grasp the bigger picture. When we are willing to look at the big picture and let go of judgment, we can find the parts that we played in the drama more easily. Touching upon times when we have been the persecutor allows us to open the door to forgiveness. When that happens we can let go of judgments and anger towards others and ourselves. Forgiveness does not mean that we condone the actions of those who have hurt us, or condone our own actions; it simply means that we forgive and release the energy.

When teaching I will often hear, *"Maybe the child who is being abused today by his father was his father's abuser in a past life.*

Maybe he deserves what he's getting." The question t
"Should we just let abuse go?" My answer is that, althc
be true that the victim was the persecutor of yesterday, now is time
to become conscious and to stop the pattern of abuse. If we do not
do this, the karmic wheel of pain and suffering continues. If we do
not assist the victim in waking up to the greater picture and moving
into healing and forgiveness, then we enable that person to remain
disempowered and enmeshed in the abusive pattern. If we do not
extend compassion to the persecutor, we support them to continue
the same pattern. I need to stress here that forgiveness is not the focus
of this work. The focus is to be present, without judgment, so that
the client can experience the feelings, release the energy, reclaim the
self and heal. When healing happens, forgiveness naturally happens
to follow.

It is important to remember that past life memories are no excuse
for present-life behavior. In other words, *"I don't have to make
amends because I just found out that you killed me in another lifetime
and I'm only giving you back what you deserve,"* is not what this is
about. This type of thinking only perpetuates the karmic wheel. In
becoming aware of the whole picture we become accountable to our
spirit so that we can live in our highest place of integrity.

Frederick

❧

"There are treasures beyond compare in the ocean.
If you seek safety, stay ashore."

~ Sufi saying

Frederick first came to me because of the hate that he felt for his stepsister. Frederick had been in pursuit of a spiritual path for many years and was quite aware of the power of thought, forgiveness, and extending love to others. He had tried every means known to him, but still could not resolve the feelings of hatred that he felt toward this woman. Although their relationship had seen difficult times, he could not think of anything that warranted such intense feelings of hate and mistrust. Here was a man who knew the consequences of holding onto such feelings and yet felt powerless to release them.

Frederick and I decided to do a past life regression to find out how his soul and the soul of his stepsister Julie might be connected. The intention was also to release any contracts that might have been made between them. During this regression, Frederick was surprised to find that they had been lovers in a previous lifetime. He had been a woman at that time, and she a man. *She* (the present day Frederick) was very much in love, but her lover, the present day Julie, betrayed her by having many affairs. Their relationship finally ended when the lover killed her (Frederick). The last thoughts as spirit left her body were thoughts of revenge and hatred. These thoughts and feelings were carried on a cellular level into this present lifetime.

When Frederick went into that place where spirit goes between lives, he found that he and Julie's spirits were very connected and that there was great love between them. Frederick's soul had decided that, for it's greater learning about love and compassion, it needed to experience betrayal by a loved one. Although Julie's soul was reluctant to play out this drama, the agreement was made. When Frederick was able to feel the love for this soul and was able to see that this drama was set up for his own soul's growth and learning, he was able to release the energy of anger and revenge that he was carrying. For the first time, he was able to enter into a place of true forgiveness and harmony with his stepsister.

During this session, Frederick could feel the release and freedom from hate in his body. As the tears flowed from his eyes, and a smile turned the corner of his lips, he could feel the warm energy of love filling him more deeply then he had ever felt it before.

This was a very exciting session for me to participate in. Here again is a wonderful example of how our soul decides upon a lesson to be learned during a physical incarnation. The assistance from other souls is elicited; we don our bodysuits, and begin the drama, never remembering that we were the ones who called the players together.

This wonderful story shows how true forgiveness brings healing to us. It nourishes our soul and every cell of our physical being with love. It allows our energy to come home to us. This is why Jesus said, *"Love your enemies."* Until we can reach that place of love and forgiveness, the body, mind, and spirit suffer. If we want to feel loved and filled with the essence of God/Spirit then we must be willing to love and forgive ourselves as well as others.

Ann & Danny

∽

"Love one another and you will be happy. It's as simple and as difficult as that."

~ Michael Leunig

Past life contracts are often made at the time of death. The last feelings, thoughts, or words that we express carry over into our next lifetime. Contracts concerning relationships could be:

I will never leave you again.

I'll always take care of you.

I'll get you back if it's the last thing I do!

I will do anything you ask, just so you will never leave me.

I will always love you.

These words and intentions may come from love, guilt, grief, or a combination of feelings. They tie the soul to the contract even in times where there is abuse. When a contract is in place, a normally logical person may act in illogical ways that are confusing to themselves and to others who know them. For example, a woman who may be genuinely loving and caring for her children may put up with the abuse of herself and them from a man who, *always promises to change*. She may pack up and leave only to return to his apologies and a repeat pattern of abuse. Her friends may try to help, she may go to counseling to resolve father issues, early abuse issues, self-esteem issues, all the issues she can find, but the magnetic attraction to this man remains.

Imagine a strong, outgoing man who does well in the business world, but in his personal life allows himself to be manipulated and used by a woman whom he plans to marry. His friends may see this, talk to him about it, and even get angry with him. They may be confused as to why he will not listen to them or see for himself what is happening. He is the only one who feels the pull of the contract and even though he does not know it on a conscious level, he is bound to his agreement, and so goes the story of Ann and Danny.

Ann and Danny were lovers. They had felt a strong connection at their first meeting five years ago at a college dance. Danny was handsome and well liked by his peers. There were many girls who would have loved to date him, but from the first moment they met he only *had eyes* for Ann. He was the perfect boyfriend: considerate, giving, true, and always there when Ann needed him,-and she needed him a lot. Ann seemed to have no consideration for Danny. She flirted with other boys even when they were out together and continued to do this even though she knew how much it hurt Danny. She was demanding and belittled him often when they were out with friends. No one could understand what he saw in her - well, maybe she was beautiful, but her attitude surely wasn't. None of Danny's friends liked her; they just put up with her for his sake. Danny always defended Ann and their relationship. He'd say things like, *"That's the way she is, she doesn't mean any harm,"* or *"It's different when we're alone together."*

They became engaged. Danny began to have doubts and attempted to break off the engagement several times, but each time it was the same. Ann would cry and profess her love for Danny, make promises that she wouldn't keep, and always, somehow, make him feel guilty. He would end up apologizing for his behavior and bring her gifts to make up. As their marriage date grew closer, Danny became more depressed until he seemed unable to make even simple decisions. This angered Ann and she threatened to leave. Although this break was what Danny knew was right and exactly what he needed, he could not bear the thought of losing her. Finally, he decided to seek help through hypnotherapy.

As Danny drifted back in time, he found himself passing through the veil between lifetimes and entering a past life where, to his surprise, he was inhabiting the body of a woman. This woman was from a very wealthy family and had many suitors. One in particular was exceedingly fond of her and succeeded in winning her hand in marriage. Although this husband was very caring and good to her, she had affairs with other men and humiliated him in public. When Danny looked into the eyes of this husband, he recognized the eyes of Ann. As this lifetime progressed and Danny (then the wife) grew older, the husband (Ann), finally no longer able to withstand the abuse, called for a divorce and married a woman with whom he spent the rest of his life. The now divorced woman (Danny) lost her money and her beauty. She grew old alone and regretted having forced her husband away by her cruelty. She watched her ex-husband's reputation grow and saw that many loved him. At the time of death she said, *"If I could only have him back I would do anything I could to make him happy."*

Danny began to cry as he saw the contract he had made. The way Ann treated him probably had to do with anger that she carried over from that time and she may have possibly set up a contract of her own that claimed revenge on Danny for the humiliation she had suffered in that life. After Danny witnessed his death in the previous life and found the contract, I asked him to leave his body and go to the place where spirit dwells to find his soul's lesson from that lifetime. His lesson was to value the heart above material wealth and social position. Danny had learned well. In his current life, although successful in the *real* world, his heart always came first.

I asked if he would like to go back and change anything in this past life. Danny said, *"Yes,"* and went back to when he was born into that lifetime. With all the wealth his family had, he never received the love and appreciation that he desired. It was through this that he had learned to manipulate others and lose respect for material wealth. Danny imagined himself to be born into that family again, only this time he was loved and nurtured. He gained appreciation of himself and others. When he married, he honored the relationship because he now honored himself. When he followed this new life to its end, he and his partner were happy together and left that lifetime with a feeling of love for each other.

Can a past life experience be rewritten like a theater script? And, if so, does this change the present? I believe that the answer to both questions is yes. Whether it is with inner child work or past life regression, our bodies, like computers, hold and are fundamentally affected by programmed memory. Memory is an energy that is stored in the cells. If this energy, or memory, is changed, the self seems to function in a different way. Changing the energy also causes a shift on the Etheric Plane, which in turn, affects others who are involved with the shift we make.

In the case of Danny and Ann, the energy shift led the couple to begin counseling. They postponed the wedding and made a commitment to work on their relationship. For the first time, Ann was willing to look at her behavior and understand that she needed counseling as well as Danny if they were to create a healthy relationship. Ann and Danny did marry two years later and continue their commitment to each other.

Ann and Danny were able to resolve their differences, respect each other, and commit to their relationship. However, there could have been a different ending. Danny could have released himself from the previous life's contract and Ann could have been furious with the energy shift. She could have tried harder to manipulate him and gain revenge. If this had occurred, Danny, now free from guilt, would have been able to leave the relationship and move on with his life. There are many possibilities. The key is that once he made the shift, whatever followed would bring healthy resolution for him.

Ruth

"Happiness is not a destination. It is a method of life."
~ Burton Hills

Sometimes the soul connections and contracts we make keep us in relationships that are illogical and dysfunctional. An example of this is the story of Ruth and Andrew.

Ruth left her relationship with Andrew several times, and each time it was the same story. There would be an episode of physical abuse and degrading language that caused her to feel stupid and worthless. Ruth would pack her bags and vow to not come back, but after only a few days, her feelings of guilt would become so overwhelming that she would return with apologies and promises to be a better wife.

This scenario repeated itself at regular intervals, and even though Ruth received support from her family and friends to leave Andrew, she could not stay away from him. Finally, in desperation, she went to a therapist and became involved in a women's group. Although this gave support and insight into her co-dependency issues, she was still unable to break away. When I first met Ruth she was experiencing great emotional pain. She felt crazy because her logical self told her to leave the relationship, but her addiction to Andrew compelled her to stay.

We began a past life regression session that took Ruth to Victorian England. She was the daughter of a poor farmer and had experienced a difficult life. At about age eighteen she fell in love with a man who worked at a livery stable in a nearby village. Their courtship was passionate and there was a deep, heartfelt connection between them.

They married, but times were difficult and their life was a financial struggle. One day, Ruth a beautiful woman with a bright, outgoing personality was noticed by a passing baron, about fifteen years her senior. He wooed her secretly and in a short time promised to marry her and share his great wealth if she would consent to divorcing her husband and marrying him. Although this was difficult, both because of the times and because of the love she had for her husband, Ruth eventually gave in and became the baron's wife.

At first she enjoyed her fine clothes, jewels and home, but soon she became disenchanted with her new way of life. She had never loved the baron and continued to mourn for the relationship she had left. During one visit back home to see her ailing father, she heard news of her first husband. He had been so hurt by her rejection that he started to drink heavily and within the year had hung himself.

Ruth's sense of loss, grief, and guilt were overwhelming. Her heart became as cold as steel and she refused to allow love in. After the baron died she became a bitter and lonely widow whose wealth brought no happiness. At the time of her death in that lifetime she vowed that if she were ever again given the chance to be with the man whom she loved, she would endure all and never leave him. The man, of course, was Andrew, and the illogical guilt that Ruth experienced came from her past life guilt, which she had carried with her to the grave.

During the session, after her time of death, I asked Ruth if there were anything that she would like to change. She said *yes*, and returned to the time when the baron asked her to marry him. She professed her love for her husband, made the decision to stay with him and rejected the baron's advances. The couple worked hard and succeeded in making a modest, but adequate living. They had two fine children and lived a contented and happy life. In this changed lifetime, her children and grandchildren surrounded Ruth at her time of death. Her husband had passed on the year before. This time she left her body in peace and looking forward to being united with him. With this change, the past life contract was dissolved.

In this life, Andrew also carried with him the unconscious past life memory of being betrayed. Although he loved Ruth, the anger and hurt from that life spilled over and contaminated his feelings for her in this life. The love he felt for Ruth, followed by his abuse of her, left Andrew feeling guilty and out of control. His way of dealing with the problem was to drink; the same method of coping he had used in that previous lifetime.

Ruth noticed an energetic shift after our session. She knew that, even though she loved Andrew, she could now take care of herself and leave the marriage for good. With her shift in energy an interesting thing happened with Andrew. He apparently felt the shift in Ruth and sensed that she was free, too. One night, a week after the session, Andrew uncharacteristically burst into tears and said that he wanted to begin therapy, something he had previously been unwilling to do. Several years have passed now and Ruth and Andrew continue to learn and grow in their relationship. The abuse and drinking have stopped and they are living happily together.

When I teach hypnotherapy classes and work with clients, I always say that the reason to do this work is for your own understanding and healing, *not* to change someone else. A side benefit is that communication at this deep level often affects the other person as well. Unconsciously, we are connected to the energy of those around us, and that connection is strongest with those who are closest to. I feel that it was for this reason that Andrew felt the shift in Ruth. This caused fear that would lose her again, and this fear compelled him to express his emotions and seek counseling. Because of Ruth's experience with hypnotherapy, Andrew also came to see me so that he could clear the energy he was holding from that lifetime. After his release of the anger and pain he was holding, he was free to live with Ruth in present time. It is always a joy and incredible experience to work with couples in this way.

Section IV
Personal Soul Contracts

❧

"Sometimes, it seems to me, that in this absurdly random life there is some inherent justice in the outcome of personal relationships. In the long run, we get no more than we have been willing to risk giving."

~ Sheldon Kopp

Recognizing Personal Soul Contracts

∾

"There is one thing one has to have, either a soul that is cheerful by nature, or a soul made cheerful by work, love and knowledge."
~ Fredrich Neitzsche

I have spoken about contracts that exist between souls and now would like now to discuss personal soul contracts; the contracts we make with our own soul before entering the physical plane. Such contracts are also made for the purpose of healing and awakening. We may call upon other souls to help us achieve our goal, but the main contract here is with the self.

Personal soul contracts can often be recognized in repeated patterns. If a person continually experiences a pattern of events, that persists, even though the players change, a personal soul contract may exist. This contract may stem from present-life childhood trauma or past life trauma. For example, if a woman finds herself being raped repeatedly, there may be a soul contract to learn about rape and forgive herself for times in a past life where she may have participated as a rapist. Or these experiences may be a way of her soul calling her to heal beliefs about being a victim and taking her power. Someone who repeats the pattern of being fired, or experiencing difficult managers, may have been the one in the past who treated employees or slaves unfairly. The person who always *falls in love* only to find the object of their attention leaving them for someone else may have carelessly broken hearts in another lifetime. Looking for what underlies such patterns is not about justification or blame, it is about gaining under-standing and freedom. It may be easier to think of ourselves as the

ctim, but in reality, over lifetimes there is not one among
nocent.

...mic wheel is ever turning. We may get away with *bad* behavior in one lifetime, but that behavior will follow us into our next incarnation. This is what the biblical statement *"Do unto others as you would have them do unto you"* means. The purpose of a personal soul contract is not for punishment, but for attaining higher awareness. When we experience all things, we find understanding, compassion, forgiveness, love of self, and love of others. Past life work has taught me about soul contracts. As we remember more of our past lives, we see that we have been it all (male, female, black, white, gay, straight, victim, persecutor), and done it all. When we realize this, there is less room to hate and to judge others and less room to hate and judge ourselves. Through awareness and understanding of our contracts, we can stop repeating the old patterns and get off the karmic wheel.

When a pattern repeatedly occurs with one specific person, it is likely that a soul contract with that person is involved. Personal soul contracts, however, are a little different, as they are not made with another person, but made with oneself. Whenever you have been willing to work on healing an issue, yet no matter what you do the issue still exists, could be a sign that a personal soul contract exists. You may have read, listened to tapes, done inner child work, gone to seminars, tried traditional counseling or alternative therapies, and yet, despite all this work, the pattern or feelings *still* exist. Sure it may be better and you may have gained insights or noticed positive changes, but somewhere in your core you can still feel the pattern's pull. This is a classic sign of a personal soul contract.

If you notice yourself being continually attracted to studying a certain subject, doing a certain line of work, or working with a certain group of people, you may be experiencing the draw of a soul contract. Some of the most common issues that I have worked with concerning such contracts follow.

I teach hypnotherapy classes to people who are seeking to develop their healing skills. Ironically, I frequently have sound students in our classes who are studying hypnotherapy, but who have made past life contracts to stay away from doing any type of healing work.

You might ask, *"Why are they taking these classes?"* The answer is simple. Their souls are drawn to this work and they have the ability to be healers, but they have forgotten the contract on a conscious level. The two most common reasons that I have found for such contracts are the abuse of power and persecution. They were guided to taking the class because their soul is seeking release of these contracts and desires them to release the contract and awaken their healing abilities. It seems that many healers who left this work in previous lives, are being called forth to assist on the planet at this time.

If a contract to stay away from healing work was made it can be recognized by several behaviors. Among these are:

The person continues to take classes but never feels ready to do the work.

The person wants to take classes in healing but always has an excuse why they can't.

The person sets up a healing practice, but charges fees too low to support him/herself.

In all the above examples the people involved try to convince themselves and others that they have tried their best, but it just hasn't worked for them. This gives them permission to retreat back into the safety of the *real* world. The following story of Mary provides a perfect example of this:

Mary

"Walk with those seeking truth: Run from those who think they found it."

~ Deepak Chopra

Mary was a massage therapist who wanted to incorporate the use of herbs and flower remedies into her work. As soon as she started taking a class on the healing use of herbs she began to discount herself and her abilities. She also became fearful of being able to do this work and was thinking about returning to her previous job as a legal secretary. Mary had always been a confident, successful and independent person who went after what she wanted. These new fears were confusing and unfamiliar to her.

Because of Mary's past successes and self-confidence, I had the feeling that this current issue might be connected to a personal soul contract made in a past lifetime. Mary wanted to explore this concept and we began a session with this in mind. In the session, Mary soon found herself living in a small cottage, in what appeared to be Seventeenth Century England. She was a wise woman and many people from a nearby village traveled to her home to receive the healing benefits of her work. Because she lived alone and rarely went into the town, the people were somewhat frightened of her. She grew, found, and dried her own herbs and flowers. She loved doing this and often spent days out in the forests and fields gathering her supplies. She was in contact with the devas who lived in her glen and regularly communicated with them.

It was a very peaceful life until a group of riders came into town talking about the devil and witchcraft. This frightened the villagers and they told the men about Mary. The men convinced the townsfolk that she was one of these witches and had been poisoning their souls. They led some of the people, carrying torches, to Mary's cottage. After shouting things like, *"witch!"* and *"devil woman!"* they set her home on fire. Terrified, Mary burned to her death. When Mary and I went back to that moment just before her death, Mary realized that she had made a contract to never do this work again.

During the next part of our session, I asked Mary if there were anything that she would like to change in that past life. She did not know what to do, so we asked her higher self to show her. She was brought back into that lifetime, only this time she did not do her work in secret. She made friends with the local pastor and two of the wealthiest and most respected families in the village. She educated them about the value of herbs and spoke of how they were gifts from God, and how He guided her to use them. She went into town weekly, attending service at the local church and became well liked by the townspeople. This time, when the men rode into town the people did not even think of Mary when the men spoke of the evil of witches. There was no energy in this town for these men so they rode on their way.

Mary next went to that place where spirit lives and asked what the learning was for her from that time. She was told that the lesson was to awaken to the importance of including others. Instead of *doing* things to people, it was time for her to educate them and assist them in their healing process. The energy change that occurred in reliving the past life allowed Mary to relax and enjoy her present-day study of herbal and flower remedies.

From this session, it is easy to understand how Mary could be successful when pursuing a variety of healing modalities, but became frightened as soon as she began exploring herbal remedies. Her soul had drawn her to the herbal remedy class as a way of waking her up to receive the lesson she needed and do the work in which she was skilled. Instead of meeting the fear, Mary could have given in to it and returned to her old job where she probably would have never felt fulfilled and, perhaps, may have even become ill or depressed.

The Money Contract

"Heroes take journeys, confront dragons, and discover the treasure of their true selves."

~ Carol Pearson

Money is another key area in which personal contracts create patterns. I have worked with many people who have abused power and material wealth in past lives, and, because of this, have made contracts keep this from happening again. Sometimes these people are born into the belief system that money is dirty, bad, unholy, or corrupt and not important to them. This is a great protective system because it allows the individual to forego the desire for material wealth for virtuous and holy reasons. This works until the individual decides one day, that s/he wants greater abundance in their life. Maybe it's time to get out of the low-income bracket, travel, have a nice home, pretty things, fine clothes, or other things that money can buy. At this point, a little voice inside comes out with something like: *"How selfish. You should be happy with what you have.... look at all the poverty in the world, you should be ashamed."*

A frequent next step is to buy books on creating prosperity, to take classes, or engage in therapy. Through such means we can examine our issues around self-worth and deserving and may even come to the place of saying, *"Yes, I am worthy. I do deserve abundance."* But, then the money doesn't come, or it comes into our lives only to be stopped by some unforeseen event of self-sabotage. A feeling of frustration usually follows with thoughts such as, *"No matter what I do, nothing seems to work."* If you find this or a similar scenario in your life, it might be a good time to check and see if you may have made a past life contract regarding wealth. If there is a hidden fear that having wealth will lead to abuse of power, that fear will kick in and take over as soon as money begins to accumulate.

Let's take the story of George. George was born into a middle-class family and was always told what a good boy he was because he rarely asked his parents for anything. He always seemed happy with whatever he had and this pleased his parents. When his siblings persisted in making demands of their parents to buy them things, his mother would always say, *"Why can't you be like your brother? He never asks for anything."* So George grew up and became attached to this *virtue*. George thought of himself as pious and was glad that he did not succumb to the *ways of the world*. This made him feel as if he were better than his brothers, sisters, and everyone else who concerned themselves with material goods. Life went on this way until George was thirty-two and his soul decided that it was time for him to become conscious. His wake up call came through a young woman named Margaret.

Margaret was pretty, bright, and talented. She appreciated George's simple life until they seriously began to consider the possibility of marriage. Although Margaret valued the balance George brought into her life, he didn't reciprocate. He began criticizing her about how she spent her money. This created a friction in their relationship and Margaret decided that although his simple way of living was endearing, she wanted to have nice things, travel, and provide well for any children she might have. Margaret was ready to break off the engagement when George came to see me with the hope that hypnotherapy might help him to save his relationship.

Our first step was to do inner-child work. This enabled George to recognize his talents and strengths while letting go of his attachment to virtuous poverty. After our second session, we decided that it might be helpful to see if there was a past life connection to George's issue of pious poverty.

In this next session, George found himself in Egypt. He was an aide to the king and took delight in bedecking himself with fine clothes, gold and jewels. His responsibility, it seemed, was to oversee a large group of slaves who were constructing a building for the king. Each day George would ride out in a wagon-type vehicle, which he described as having two large wheels and being pulled by a team of horses. It was very hot and the slaves worked very hard. George was proud of how they stopped their work to bow when he came by. He wanted them to admire his elegant wardrobe and know that the king favored him. He had no compassion for the slaves and spoke harshly to the captains and he took pleasure in watching the slaves beaten.

I had George go through this lifetime, learning whatever was important for him to know. He came to a scene where he had wandered far out into the fields alone. He felt himself fall as his foot sunk into a hole and his ankle turned. There was great pain and he could not get up. At that moment, a small group of slaves came into view, carrying a heavy stone. George waved his arm and demanded that they come and pick him up. He saw the slaves carry the stone toward him, then felt the crushing sensation as they dropped it over his body. Going back to that incident just before death, George felt his own terror, but he also noticed the faces of those men with the stone. For the first time he felt *their* pain. For an instant he regretted his actions and made the contract to never abuse wealth and power in that way again.

George did not want to go back and change the story. What he needed was to meet with this past life part of himself and do forgiveness work. As George held this part, cried, and forgave himself while I did energy work over his body. I prayed that the cells be released of the pain; yet keep the knowledge and compassion that they gained from the past life. This was quite a difficult session for George and two weeks later he was still processing all that had happened.

George noticed a shift in his life after this last session. He found that he was kinder to himself and that his relationship with Margaret was better. He shared the story of his session with her and she was open to his experience. Today they are communicating much better in their relationship, and George has even purchased the occasional special gift for Margaret.

Through self-forgiveness George was able to re-lease his contract from the past life and understand that he can be materially abundant and compassionate and loving at the same time. To reinforce this under-standing, George chooses to donate money and carpentry skills to a shelter for the homeless. He now sees money as an energy that can be used to both care for him and to help others.

Money issues are commonly rooted in personal soul contracts. I see this revealed again and again with clients and students.

John and the AIDS Virus

～

"You must be the change you wish to see in the world."
~ Mahatma Gandhi

I also see soul contracts played out through illness. The following story, of a man whom I will call John, is a profound example of this.

John had developed *kaposi's sarcoma*, a cancer of the skin that can occur in people with AIDS. John's holistic doctor suggested hypnotherapy as a therapeutic option, and so John sought me out. After explaining the process of Spiritual Hypnosis to John, he decided that he wanted to explore any message the AIDS virus had for him.

To begin our session, I took John into a medium trance state where he soon found himself riding a horse into a castle courtyard. The scene was clearly that of Europe in the Middle Ages. As he approached the heavy stonewalls he felt the excitement of returning home after being away at war. The massive wooden gates were open, as if in anticipation of his return, and as he rode into the center of the courtyard he noticed a young woman with a baby in her arms running out to meet him. She was his wife and the child was their daughter. He reached down and picked up the little girl, and as he did so his wife exclaimed, *"Everyone has the plague here, even our daughter!"* Upon hearing these words, John threw the baby back into his wife's arms, turned his horse around and galloped away from that place.

He rode and rode until he was exhausted. Both he and his horse needed rest and water, so finding a small pond, he stopped and got down from his horse. As he bent down over the water, John saw the mark of the plague reflected back in his own face. In fear and despair, he took up his sword and plunged it through his heart.

One of the most powerful moments of past life regression work comes when the person recalls the time of death as this it the moment when we often make our soul contract for the next lifetime. I asked John to go back to the time just before he plunged the sword into his heart and notice what his last words or thoughts were. What came to him was; *"I will come back for another plague and this time I won't run!"*

John did come back for another plague, AIDS, and this time he didn't run. He contracted the HIV virus very early on and, instead of taking the recommended drug called AZT, he focused on natural healing re-sources. He talked to his friends about natural choices and watched as, one-by-one they took AZT, became sicker and finally died from this plague. He found that instead of people being open and willing to learn from him, they directed their anger towards him because he would not take AZT.

John's Spiritual Hypnosis session was just one piece of his healing program. Through our session, he became conscious of his soul's contract and the reason why he made this contract. Because of his commitment to healing and his positive outlook on life, John is healthy and living a happy and productive life these many years later. He has told me that he is no longer HIV+ and he no longer associates himself with having HIV/AIDS.

Judy

"Thousands of candles can be lighted from a single candle and the life of the candle will not be shortened. Happiness never decreases by being shared."

~ Buddha

Soul contracts provide us with profound lessons. When we become conscious of these contracts and the events leading to them, we gain great insight and are able to break the patterns that bind us to the past, and are free to move forward. Other people are nearly always part of our growth, and sometimes souls gather in family clusters that support individual soul contracts. This was the case for Judy.

Judy, a close friend of mine, had been keeping a secret for many years. Finally she was willing to share this secret and feel the shame that went with it. Many years ago, when Judy was a young woman, and the mother of four children, she had gotten involved in an abusive relationship. Her two youngest children were born from that relationship. When Judy decided to leave the relationship, her husband threatened to kill her and all of the children. Judy bravely took the children and moved into a friend's house despite these threats, but since the husband knew where Judy worked, she never felt safe and was always afraid that he would find them. As can be imagined, this was a terrifying time for her.

Judy remained in contact with her husband's sister who relayed messages between them. One such message from him was that if Judy let his sister adopt his two children he would leave her and her other two children alone. His sister, who wanted to have children but could not have them, was happy to agree to this arrangement. Judy liked the sister and felt that this woman could offer the children a more stable and secure life than she could provide at the time, so she agreed to the adoption. Even though she felt this was the best thing for the children, the decision was extremely difficult and brought her much pain and shame. Her son, Jack Jr., was four and her daughter, Gail, was three at the time. Judy cried as she shared this story and related how little Jack had clung to her crying, *"Take me home mommy!"*

Judy had carried this pain within her heart for nearly twenty-five years. She felt great shame for not being able to better care for these children whom she dearly loved, and even greater shame for giving them up.

Judy and I had become friends through our study of Alchemical Hypnotherapy, and we are both committed to doing our personal work. She asked that I use her real name because she says that she kept this secret long enough, and now, through her prayers and this work, healing has come. I feel honored to share her story, a rich example of how beings come together to complete individual personal soul contracts, in this book. Judy's contract and that of her children, was revealed in our session together.

About two years ago, Judy began to search for her children. She paid an agency a finder's fee and waited. She wanted to know how they were and to begin communication with them, if they were willing. She waited for several months and had only received one envelope containing nothing she found useful. One day, during a hypnotherapy class that she was teaching, the students broke up into practice groups and by *coincidence* it turned out that Judy had the opportunity to teach a co-induction (where two people use their voices simultaneously to induce trance) piece with herself as the subject. They asked if there was anything special that she wanted to work on and she said, *"No"*. Then, all of a sudden the tears came, and for the first time she shared her story. During the session, an inner guide told her that she must do another session about this before being reunited with her children, and the guide suggested that she do the session with me.

Judy lived in Spokane and a few months following that session with her students I flew out to her school to teach a hypnotherapy class. I always left for home as soon as class was finished, but this time I decided to stay one extra night so that Judy and I would have time for a session exchange. This occurred a few months after Judy's guide had suggested that she receive a session from me and at that time I was unaware of this suggestion.

When the time came for Judy's session, she told me the story of her children and asked that the focus of her session be on finding them. As she went into the trance state, Judy entered into a past life story in which she and a man were walking across a desert. He had no covering for his feet and Judy never offered to share what she had with him. The man's feet were badly blistered and he was in great pain when they finally walked into a town. The townsfolk pitied the man and took care of him while they chastised Judy for her lack of compassion. In watching this scenario Judy felt waves of sadness and shame move through her body. Her guide told her that this was one of many lifetimes in which she had been shamed and that her soul contract for this lifetime was to release the shame. Her guide went on to say that she and her two youngest children had made an agreement to assist each other in healing deep issues in this current lifetime. She was told that both these children carried issues of abandonment into this lifetime. I can just imagine these three souls talking before coming down into the physical plane. *"I want to heal this shame I've been carrying around for lifetimes."* and *"We want to heal this abandonment issue."* Then, *"Hey, I have an idea! Why don't you be our mom? Then you can leave us so we can feel abandoned and you can feel the shame? Deal?"* *"Deal."* And so, the contract was made. Each soul had its personal contract and commitment to healing, as well as an agreement to assist the others with their individual contracts.

After learning of the contract agreements, Judy saw a bird's nest full of baby birds, their necks stretched out and beaks open. Immediately she noticed how drained she felt, always giving to her children, grandchildren, husband, students, etc. She said, *"Everybody always wants something from me!"* As she got closer to the birds she was shocked to hear that what they were really crying was, *"Leave us alone, leave us alone!"*

In that moment, Judy saw how the shame she had been holding was driving her to do everything, and be everything for everyone.

It was this force, rather than outside circumstances that compelled her to take care of others. She imagined letting the birds take care of themselves and watched how even a fall from the nest created an opportunity for growth, an opportunity that they wouldn't have had if she had stepped in to help.

Judy now understood that the drama she lived in this life was agreed upon before incarnation and that the experience provided the opportunity for powerful healing for everyone concerned. Judy was able to communicate with the souls of Gail and Jack. She shared her feelings of love for them and felt that love returned. She was then able to release the shame that had taken up a large portion of the center of her body, all the way from her heart to her power center just above the navel. In its place she brought in the piece of herself that had left to make room for the shame. This piece had to do with self-love and as the energy of self-love filled the space where shame once lived, Judy felt a deep sense of peace and love for herself and for her children. This was a very sacred moment of deep spiritual, emotional, and cellular healing that unfolded in her life in a beautiful way.

Judy had been upset with the agency she had hired to locate her children. She felt that they had only given her information that she could have accessed herself on the Internet and she was going to stop payment to them because they hadn't provided the promised service. About a week after our session Judy was searching for her agency account number in order to cancel their services when she discovered a paper she had not seen before. On this paper was the phone number of a contact person for her daughter. Even though she had looked through the information in the envelope when it arrived several months earlier, she had never seen this piece. Spirit works in marvelous ways.

Judy immediately called the contact number on the paper and was soon speaking with her daughter. They had a joyful, tearful reunion over the phone. Judy learned that her daughter had been searching for her for about five years, but had finally given up after using a Ouija board. The letters of the Ouija board had spelled out, *"Stop looking. She will find you."* (The Ouija board is only a tool that, when used with right intention, allows our subconscious, Higher Self, and Spirit to communicate with us.)

As I write this, Judy is preparing for a family re-union. Gail, Gail's husband, and a grandson whom Judy has never met will be coming *home*. Gail will be reunited with her mom and two sisters and will meet a new dad, brothers-in-law and several nephews. Judy has now also spoken with her son, Jack, and his wife, and they are looking forward to the time when they will be together. Though there was great pain in the past, Judy's, Gail's and Jack's honesty and willingness to communicate has brought great healing to the present.

The Thread of Life
(advanced past-life technique)

"Keep love in your heart. A life without it is like a sunless garden
when the flowers are dead. The consciousness of loving
and being loved brings a warmth and richness to life
that nothing else can bring."

~ Oscar Wilde

Many years ago I was working with a client who had abandonment issues that he couldn't seem to release no matter how much attention he had, or love there was in his life. This happened early on in my career as a hypnotherapist and I didn't know quite what to do when we arrived at the place in his past life session where I asked if he would like to change anything, and he answered that he couldn't.

I had done what I was taught and it didn't work. Now what to do? One of the reasons I love this work is that is it so spiritual. I may not have known what direction to take, but I was sure Divine Guidance did, so I said a prayer and giving the session to God, I waited. As the subconscious mind does not track time, this work allows the therapist to be silent for a few moments and connect on the Angelic, or Higher Plane. Inspiration came, and I suggested to the young man who lay before me that he go to a life before this one, when he had the same issue. He did, and I was thrilled, until again when we reached that point of changing the past, and again he said he couldn't. Well, I thought, it worked once, so why not again, and he went back to the third life, repeated the pattern and went on to the fourth life.

This time he saw himself being carried by a young woman in a long dress down to a river where she put him into a small, round basket and sent him floating down the river. He could sense the tall reeds blowing gently in the wind on the riverbank and could feel the rocking of the basket on the water. Eventually, hungry he began to cry, and finally was noticed and picked out of the river by an old woman. He was taken to her home and cared for, but as he grew, he was told by those in his new family of how he was found, and so he always wondered where he came from and why he was sent away. Despite the love he received, he always felt separate from this family and spent his life alone, never marrying or having children. At his time of death he made the contract with himself that he would rather be alone, a now familiar pattern, than to risk being abandoned again.

Finally he was able to change this life. He returned to the place where he was put in the basket and found that his mother, although grieved to send her little son away, had done this to save him. It seems that there was a decree and soldiers were killing the male babies in the village and surrounding area. The mother hoped that her baby would be carried far enough away and spared his life. When he heard this, and felt her love, so great that she would make such a sacrifice, he broke down into tears and the wall that encrusted his heart melted away. He felt love for this woman, and as he told her the story of her child, she wept for joy, for she had never known what had become of him. The client did not need to change anything else from the lifetime, his heart was open to love, and that was all he needed.

I then asked him to go to the previous life to see if he would like to change anything, and he replied; *"No, it has been changed already."* The same was true for the first two lives and when we future paced (a technique for seeing how the future will be affected by the work done in the session) he felt a warmth and openness in his heart, along with a sense of belonging that he had not previously experienced in this life.

I felt excited about this session, as I had been given a new tool for past life work. Since that time I have suggested at the start of every past-life session that the client go to the very first lifetime where the issue began. Healing the time when the energy was first introduced into the cellular structure allows the thread to be pulled in the fabric of lifetimes. The thread connects through every lifetime, so releasing it at the beginning releases it all the way through to the present time.

A Personal Journey

∾

"There are only two ways to live your life. One is as though nothing is a miracle. The other is as if everything is."
~ Albert Einstein

I love the way Caroline Myss talks about how we make our soul plan and then descend onto the physical plane with our angel hollering out after us, *"But you're not going to remember any of this!"* Being such a visual person, that image makes me smile as my heart resonates with its truth. By becoming conscious of and understanding our soul contracts, we can find the lessons that our soul agreed to learn and release the thoughts of anger, blame, betrayal, guilt and shame that we hold towards others and ourselves. We can find forgiveness, peace, and love.

Though we may find great pain connected with past life contracts, the reason for those contracts is not to make us suffer, but to help us become the powerful, talented, compassionate, abundant beings that we are. Our lessons show us many aspects of ourselves and of humanity. Our willingness to do this work allows us to become whole and truly live from our heart center.

In doing this work I have naturally been curious to explore my personal soul contracts. Several years ago, I received a hypnotherapy session that took me back to the time of my conception in 1948. I experienced my spirit as an expanded energy that immediately felt crushed upon entering my mother's womb. There was a feeling of panic as I thought, *"I don't want to be here! I want to get out!"* This was followed by the violent sensation that I was being crushed. This sensation was so intense that my body began to contort and I could *see* large sandstone boulders rolling upon me and crushing me to death. As I further regressed, I witnessed an avalanche covering my body. In that moment, I realized that this feeling of being crushed was brought into my present-day body, however this time the crushing was emotional and spiritual rather than physical.

My soul made a contract to learn lessons that would give me the courage and strength to stand in my power and integrity without fear or shame. In the moment of this revelation, my whole life made sense. The pieces fell together and I understood how everything and everyone in my life, no matter how painful or difficult, was there to support me in attaining this goal.

As the session continued, I settled down and began to feel the excitement of moving through the birth canal. This enthusiasm quickly transformed into a deep sense of shame as my genitals emerged. Oh no! I was supposed to have been a boy! This began a series of life experiences that reinforced the shame and belief that who I was not good enough. I was shamed for being overly sensitive, for not doing the right things or acting the right way, and at nineteen I became anorexic. It was in 1968, I was in nursing school and eating disorders had not yet entered the public eye. Twiggy was in, and a girl couldn't be too thin. No one noticed that I was starving myself to death. As I look back, I see that it was the shame, lack of self-love and feeling like it was wrong to want to live my own life that was being acted out through this self-abuse.

Often I hear clients say, *"I only want to understand why this happened to me. Why was I treated this way? Why did my parents abuse me? What did I do to deserve this? Why was I abandoned?"* Personally, I don't believe that there is any excuse or reason for abuse from the physical dimension point of view and that is why looking for the reason in this dimension usually fails us. You may come to realize that abusers abused us because they were abused, but that offers little solace. Seeking the answer in this dimension can keep you looking for someone or something to blame and keep you from healing. Focusing on the *why* keeps you from opening to the lesson, reclaiming your personal power, and living your life in a full and healthy way.

Letting go and seeking the big picture may not be an easy task, in fact it probably won't be. The key for me has been to take the question beyond this physical world and into the soul's dimension. What did your soul *choose* to come into this lifetime to learn? How do the events and people in your life contribute to your soul plan? Often it seems that we receive the opposite of what we wanted. For example the soul who came to learn self-love might be abandoned, the soul who came to learn non-judgment may be discriminated against and the soul who came to learn compassion may find anguish. For myself, the feelings that I didn't fit in, I wasn't good enough, and I couldn't do or say the right thing, have given me the insight, compassion and strength to be who I am today. Without these experiences, and the people in my life who provided them, I would not have had the opportunities I needed to grow, heal and learn what was important for me. Today, I absolutely love who I am! I love my life and I can truly say that I am thankful for every situation and every person who assisted me in becoming who I am today.

I certainly didn't always feel this way. I was angry and blamed others for my pain and for my feelings that they treated me unjustly. I prayed and asked God and my guides for many years to help me to see the big picture. I believe that whenever we sincerely ask Spirit for help, that help *is* given to us. Here is one story from my life that reminds me of this.

One day I was going through a particularly rough time with Peter, whom I have spoken about earlier. He was using crystal-meth (a man-made chemical substance which is extremely destructive to both body and mind). I knew that I had become so enmeshed in his web of drugs and lies that I was losing control of my own life. I didn't know what to do. I went into Seattle to visit with a friend and all the way home prayed for a message that could help me. That night I drove into our driveway, parked my car and I walked up the stairs to the front door to find a dead hawk lying on his back, wings folded over his abdomen as if he were in prayer, and placed perfectly parallel to the door, every feather in place. I felt my angels placed him there for me and that he was the answer to my prayers. Emotion flooded through my body as I walked inside and straight to my medicine card deck to read that; *Hawk flies high near Grandfather Sun and sees across the valleys.* The message was very clear to me. I was stuck in a valley and not seeing the whole picture. I was caught up in trying to rescue this person from what I perceived to be destructive behavior, without taking into account that he might be doing exactly what he needed for his soul's growth. With a deep breath I breathed in peace, reminding myself that God, not I, was in charge. Sometimes we want things to be different for ourselves or for others. When we live in the valley and look for change on the valley floor we continue to move in limited ways, but when we fly like Hawk up to Grandfather Sun, we become aware of the big picture and of our unlimited possibilities. With this perspective comes greater understanding, less judgment, and the freedom to live our lives in ways that bring us healing, love, and joy. Each day I pray to be as close as I can be to Spirit. Each day I face the challenges presented to me and I look, as best as I am able, to see them from the soul's perspective. The more I trust that everything that happens is for good, the more I find myself finding the gifts each situation brings. As I do this, my life continues to grow more positive, peaceful, and powerful.

A concert by the Seattle Lesbian and Gay Chorus brought another opportunity for me to look from the soul's perspective. Through music and spoken word, chorus members told the story of Bobby, a twenty-year-old gay man who committed suicide because being gay was unacceptable to his family and to his church. He and his mother had prayed for several years for God to change him, and finally, unable to deal any longer with the pain; feeling like he must be completely unworthy for God not to answer his prayers, Bobby jumped from a freeway bridge into the path of a semi-truck and died instantly.

Bobby's grief-stricken mother read about her son's suffering in the journal that he left behind, and in her grief she began to question the teachings of her church while reaching out to other religious institutions to find what they were saying about being gay. In her search, she found many churches, of all denominations, that were open and affirming to gays and lesbians. She realized that it was her minister and not God who was saying it was wrong to be gay. This mother finally found the answer to why *God* wouldn't help her son. That answer was, God had made him perfect, so there was nothing to change. Bobby's mother now works with young gay and lesbian people and their families because she never wants anyone to have to go through the pain that her family experienced.

I was deeply touched when I heard how Bobby, in spirit form, visits his mother and tells her that he is proud of what she is doing. Bobby has also told his mother that he is happy where he is. There was probably not one dry eye in the audience, including mine, by the end of this story. Rather than looking at this as just a tragedy, and seeing Bobby as a victim of religious persecution, I felt that this young man and his mother were fulfilling a powerful soul contract.

From my perspective, both the connection Bobby's mother had with this particular church and the love she has for her son enables her to speak out in a powerful way. There is no one better to address the religious beliefs that spawn hate toward the LGBT (lesbian, gay, transgendered and bi-sexual community) than this woman. Through his struggle, Bobby has brought a great gift into the world at a time when LGBT people are seeking inclusion and equal rights.

There is no justification on this physical plane for the torment that Bobby was forced to endure, but on the spiritual plane, in the light of soul contracts, this young man's life was lived for a purpose. This story is a potent example of how important it is for each one of us to seek the truth and not blindly believe what we are told, even when we are told it by someone who has authority or is supposed to be an expert. Love is the answer, and any action based in fear and hate is diametrically opposed to love, to truth, and to God.

Section V
Healing Ancestral Linage

*"Every social trait labeled masculine or feminine is in truth
a human trait. It is our human right to develop and contribute
our talents whatever our race, sex, religion, ancestry, age.
Human rights are indivisible!"*

~ Wilma Scott Heide

Affects of Culture

❧

Culture is a part of The Big Picture – the reasons why you were born to your biological parents and the lessons your soul came into this physical incarnation to learn. I am writing this section after working with clients who have felt imprisoned by the beliefs of their cultures. Personally, I love to travel and learn about different cultures. The wide variety of cultural beliefs, religions, celebrations, clothing and philosophies make our world a far richer place, and I feel that people should be proud of and celebrate their cultures. Then there is a line between freedom to live your culture and imprisonment by your culture.

While teaching in China I found that young people were going through the same dilemma that we, in the United States, experienced in the sixties. Is it OK to live your own life, even if your parents disagree? Doing what pleases your parents is important in Chinese culture, and so when discussing the right one has to choose personal happiness, students would ask, *"Linda, which way is right, China or America?"* My answer was always *balance*, it is right to respect your ancestors and it is right to respect oneself. The United States of America has been a symbol of freedom in the world, and part of that freedom comes from liberation from cultural mores. While, at times, I may feel a loss for not having the same ties to culture as friends who have immigrated to my country, I also am thankful that I do not carry the burden of pleasing parents and culture that they do.

Some examples of this would be clients who have been taught mother is higher than God, and that they are a bad son or daughter if they do not sacrifice their life to please her, even if she can never be pleased and always wants more. This type of *slavery of the soul* not only suppresses the life of the child, but keeps the mother from being responsible for her own life. Any culture that promotes pleasing the parents and honoring ancestors by traditional marriage and having children, or places any cultural or religious mores above the happiness of the child, causes great suffering to children who are gay, lesbian, or who just desire a different life. The guilt that these individuals carry causes a heaviness that weighs upon the soul that desires freedom. The internal fight between cultural programming that contains the need to please parents; and the spirit that longs to live a free life can cause such conflict and torment that an individual may attempt to quell the battle within by the use of alcohol, drugs, other self-abusive action or, in extreme cases, suicide.

Although I have already touched on some of these subjects earlier in this book I felt it was important to add this section. From sessions with clients who were caught in the cultural/personal dilemma, I have learned the two-fold value of communicating with our ancestors. Through Alchemical/Spiritual Hypnotherapy I have been witness to clients who have been able to break free from internalized quilt, find freedom and come to the realization that they are a child of God, created perfectly and to live the life their spirit is calling them to live. I offer these quotations for those who suffer the guilt of placing others above ones self.

> *"Your children are not your children. They are the sons and daughters of Life's longing for itself. They come through you but not from you, and though they are with you yet they belong not to you.*
>
> *You may give them your love but not your thoughts, For they have their own thoughts. You may house their bodies but not their souls, for their souls dwell in the house of tomorrow, which you cannot visit, not even in your dreams. You may strive to be like them, but seek not to make them like you, for life*

goes not backward nor tarries with yesterday.

You are the bows from which your children, as living arrows are sent forth. The archer sees the mark upon the path of the infinite, and He bends you with His might that His arrows may go swift and far. Let your bending in the archer's hand be for gladness; for even as He loves the arrow that flies, so He loves also the bow that is stable."

– Kahlil Gibran

"Honor your Earthly Mother and keep all her laws, that your days may be long on this earth, and honor your Heavenly Father that Eternal Life may be yours in the heavens. For the Heavenly Father is a hundred times greater than all fathers by seed and by blood, and greater is the Earthly Mother than all mothers by the body. And dearer is the Son of Man (meaning each one of us) *in the eyes of his Heavenly Father and of his Earthly Mother than are children in the eyes of their fathers by seed and by blood and of their mothers by the body. And more wise are the words and laws of your Heavenly Father and of your Earthly Mother than the words and the will of all fathers by seed and by blood, and of all mothers by the body. And of more worth also is the inheritance of your Heavenly Father and of your Earthly Mother, the everlasting kingdom of earthly and heavenly life, than all the inheritances of your fathers by seed and by blood, and of your mothers by the body. And your true brothers* (and sisters) *are all those who do the will of your Heavenly Father and of your Earthly Mother, and not your brothers by blood. I tell you truly, that your true brothers in the will of the Heavenly Father and of the Earthly Mother will love you a thousand times more than your brothers by blood."*

– Jesus the Christ from the Essene Gospel of Peace

Alchemical/Spiritual Hypnotherapy allows us to see the Big Picture of our relationships and our lineage. In doing this work we can finally free ourselves from the anger, disappointment, fears, guilt and shame that is tied to those who have brought us into this world and those who have gone before us. This breaks the karmic cycle and allows us to create the life we desire. This process brings the healing to the souls of our ancestors that they have been longing for. Finally able to express regrets, share love and wisdom they learned after leaving the physical plane, and assist in helping to free and heal the ones they love, they themselves are healed and set free. I hope the stories in this section will move you and open the door to awareness of the Big Picture in your life.

Culture contains The Big Picture – the reasons why you were born to your biological parents and the lessons your soul came into this physical incarnation to learn.

Ancestors - Breaking Free

❧

"No man can cause more grief than that one clinging blindly to the vices of his ancestors."

~ William Faulkner

In this time of awakening consciousness, those of us who are willing to wake up to the bigger picture of life are now able not only to heal their own past, but also facilitate healing on a larger scale, one that reaches out to our ancestors and sends ripples through time and space. This work is extremely exciting because, beyond the feelings of fear, anger, betrayal, guilt and shame lies a whole new realm of true forgiveness, vision and oneness with all.

Many cultures and traditions, including African, Native American, Chinese and Latino honor the ancestors, and the honoring of our ancestors is an important piece of our humanity. But have you ever thought about the ancestors who have abused themselves or their family members, maybe even you? How can one honor such ancestors when they were the source of so much pain and dysfunction? To honor does not mean to agree with, to honor means to be authentic with, to share truth and provide guidance to. It is time now for us to look at the Big Picture of life, to realize our part in it and to release our own pain, shame and guilt so that our soul is free to truly forgive and help those who have caused us harm. It is also time for them to be relieved of the toxic vibrational energy that we have been holding them in, so that both they and we can be released and the wheel of karma put to rest. I am speaking here of ancestors who died in a state of anger, resentment or other lower vibrational energy. Just because a spirit leaves the body, doesn't mean that s/he is now wise, s/he may still exist in that lower vibrational state and be looking for assistance. If an ancestor was wise, kind and loving in life, s/he may be a guide for you and have much wisdom to share

When working with ancestors who have carried the line of abuse, it is important to understand that whenever we hold feelings of anger, fear, revenge or hate towards another, we are sending that same toxic vibrational energy into our own cells. It is not what happened to us in the past that poisons our life today, but our addiction to poisoning ourselves by keeping the thoughts and energy alive within us. I have worked with many clients who know this, and who have tired to forgive, but just cannot completely release the energy. Through the Alchemical process we can truly transform the lethal lead within us into the radiant golden light of spiritual awakening and peace. As an example of this, let me tell you the story of Gloria.

Gloria, a woman in her mid-forties, who had struggled much of her adult life with eating disorders, failed relationships and lack of direction, came to see me because she had been reading self-help books of a spiritual nature and decided it was time for her to do some serious personal work. She longed to be free of the past and discover her soul's purpose in this life.

During the interview I found Gloria had been physically and emotionally abused by her mother and neglected by a father who, although loved her, traveled frequently for business and so was largely absent from her life. Upon exploring her situation, it was revealed that the mother was an alcoholic caught in the familiar cycle of abusing Gloria, feeling remorse, apologizing and taking her daughter shopping, drinking to block her inner pain, and once again being abusive.

Gloria sat slightly hunched over, with fists clenched as she related the series of abuses. She interrupted the stories of abuse with statements to let me know that she was a nice person and that she understood how lonely her mother was, how her mother had been abused by her own mother and how her mother just couldn't help what she had done to Gloria. Gloria said she had read about the power of forgiveness and forgave her mother, now she just wanted to get on with her own life. Gloria's body language told me how helpless she felt (the hunched position) and how she had not forgiven her mother at all, but was still very angry with her (the clenched fists). I knew she could not truly let go of her past until she had felt and released the anger she was holding onto in the cells of her body and was able to see the Big Picture of this situation.

Alchemical Hypnotherapy combined with cellular energy work, which I refer to as *cellular housecleaning,* is deeply powerful. Following the trance induction, Gloria experienced tightness in her belly and a pain in her heart. We went down into the belly first and found a small child, Gloria at about age two, living in the core of the tightness. This little girl was in fear that if she were not perfect (which she never could be, as is true for every one of us) she would be punished. The present day, adult Gloria, was then able to go down into this scene and talk with this small, frightened child. After some time, little Gloria allowed big Gloria to hold and comfort her.

It was then that the rage came. The tightness in the belly increased from all the toxic poison that had been held there for so many years, all the unshed tears and silent screams, building like dark storm clouds ready to release their fury on the world. The screams came alive and the tears, like waterfalls, washed away the mascara (the mask) and flooded down Gloria's face carrying the toxic poisons that had been held for so long with them. I used crystal energy to help move these long-held toxins out from deep within the cells of Gloria's belly, and then I had her call in her true spirit, her true self that had to move out as it had no room to live in this cauldron of anger, guilt and shame. Now Gloria felt the rush of energy as her spirit came flooding back into her cells, taking its rightful place in her body. A miracle had happened!

Next we visited the heart, which by this time, was feeling more open, but still holding onto the pain of failed love. Of course this first failed love was Gloria's father, who had essentially abandoned her into the care of an abusive mother. Again she discovered a small child of about three years old, living in the center of her heart. This little Gloria was curled up and encased in a dark brown shell. She was afraid of being hurt and found it better to hide here than to make herself vulnerable to the outside. After some time adult Gloria and the two year old were able to convince the three year old to crack the shell and come out and into their waiting arms. Again the rage began to build, but Gloria stifled it. She loved her father and despite his neglect, he always brought her gifts when he returned home from his travels. How could she be angry with him? Wasn't it true that without him, she would have suffered even more deeply? Wasn't he the *good* parent?

Through use of the brilliant Alchemical technique of *splitting*, Gloria was able to remove the good father from the neglectful, abandoning one. She now held her good father and cried as she told him how much she loved him and adored their time together. She gave him the gift of a red jewel that represented the love she had for him and sent him on his way. After he left, Gloria looked at the bad father and her body began to tremble. Again the screams that were aching to be released from her heart found their way up through her throat and out of her mouth. Waves of sobs followed as she figuratively hit this man who had betrayed her over and over again! She could see how all her relationships with men related to this man who was supposed to have loved and protected her. Gloria was able to clear much of the old energy from her heart and she relaxed as she breathed the vibrations of love and peace into her heart.

At our next session Gloria reported that she was feeling much better. Her eating had become more moderate as she was no longer using food to ease the pain in her belly and she slept better at night.

This time we did a past life regression where Gloria entered a place where she had been the mother of her parents. That may sound strange, but often families reincarnate together as they go through the learning process their souls need. When a person becomes conscious and makes different choices, his/her soul leaves that *family* of souls and moves on to another soul family where it can continue to grow and learn new lessons. The gist of the session was that Gloria found she was not an innocent victim, but had perpetuated the abuse when she was the *parent*. Then a remarkable thing happened! Gloria was shown, at the spiritual level, how she was connected to the line of her ancestors. She saw how the abuse that she had suffered as a child in the physical life that she was now living had been passed on over and over again throughout lifetimes. At this point she realized that she had received the gift of conscious awakening and breaking of this chain of abuse was up to her.

Seeing herself as an abuser was critical. Upon the realization that she was not only victim, but also perpetrator, she was able look at her mother and grandmother with new eyes. She felt her pain and their pain and she moved into a place of deep and true forgiveness. She felt and became ONE with them. Without making one bad and another good, without the judgment and divisions she had been taught, she saw the truth. *"And the truth will set you free"* was never more appropriate than at this time. She forgave them with all her heart and they, their spirits and the spirits of other ancestors before them who were caught in this same karmic web, came forth to thank her as well. It was a very emotional time for both Gloria and myself as our bodies vibrated within love, forgiveness and the deep awareness that we are all truly ONE.

I have facilitated many such sessions and each one has been a great blessing, but the first time it happened was the most powerful for me. I realized that, yes our ancestors do have wisdom and goodness to share with us, but also they carry the pain and dysfunction that they were unwilling or unable to heal in past lifetimes and we, who are willing and able to wake up to greater consciousness are now called to help them to end their suffering, step off the karmic wheel, and release that which does not serve the highest good of humankind. The Alchemical process is like a pebble tossed into the still pool of no time, rippling out to touch and bring healing to souls throughout the ages.

The Soul Longs for Healing

∾

*"And if I forget Who I Am, you may even forget Who You Are,
and we will both be lost. Then we will need another soul
to come along and remind us both of Who We Are."*

~ Neal Donald Walsh

The above quote is taken from *The Little Soul and the Sun*, a book by Neal Donald Walsh, and one of, if not my favorite past life book. I often times share the story with clients and in groups, and many times have to hold back the tears as I do so. Written as a children's book, the profound wisdom and the beautiful pictures take the reader on a journey of inner knowing that transcends the intellect and reaches deeply into the soul. *The Little Soul and the Sun* enables the reader to see the Bigger Picture of life and the truth of self and the self of others better than anything I have read. It is simple, powerful, goes straight to the heart and is a beautiful and perfect beginning for what I am going to tell you.

Often times clients, students, or friends who know I do past life work will ask me, *"So what happens when we die?"* I don't have the answer, but I have my theories, one of which, that I gained from sessions I've witnessed, is that there are different possibilities for each soul.

I've worked with clients who had abusive parents, or parents who were loving and caring, but died when their child was young, and either way, it seems the souls of such parents, weighted down by remorse or grief, remain close to their child instead of going on and into the Light. There are too many of these stories to tell here, but let me tell you about Olivia and Samuel.

Olivia's mother died when she was seven. She had been the youngest child in a family of boys, and with five older brothers, Olivia was special to her mother who had wanted a daughter. Olivia and her mother were very close and enjoyed dressing up and doing *girl things* together. When Olivia's mother found that she had a very aggressive form of cancer, she did her best to hide this from her young daughter and succeeded with her plan so well, that she died quickly and quietly one night in her sleep. The father, who had held the stress of his wife's illness and now found himself left as a single parent with six children, became withdrawn and unable to process the death with his young daughter. Olivia felt isolated. It was felt best that she not attend the funeral and so she was even denied inclusion in the family for this last goodbye to her dear mother.

After a time Olivia became defiant, independent and had difficulty allowing her heart to fully open in any relationship. This is what brought her to me. She had become involved with a wonderful person whom she wanted to share her life with, but the feelings of wanting to push away grew with her love and she was afraid that, once again, she would push love out of her life.

Upon establishing connection with the spirit of her mother, Olivia broke down into tears – the tears that she had not been able to express from the loss of her mother and the subsequent loss of others in her life, came down in torrents. Between the heart rendering sobs she screamed out to her mother, *"Why did you leave me?"* The anger, stored in her heart for all these years, had fashioned itself into a steel gate that kept others out came crashing down, and only after Olivia had time to express herself fully to her mother, was she able to begin to take some deep breathes and begin to relax.

During the next part of the session Olivia was able to tell her mother how much she loved and missed her. She was able to once again feel the love of her mother, the love she had missed for so long. She cried as she allowed this love back into her heart and into the cells of her body. She experienced warm waves of golden light filling her and she *heard* her mother's voice telling her how she loved her and how sad she was to leave. She told Olivia of how frightened she was and how she didn't know what to do. She expresses her deep sorrow for not having told Olivia of her condition and helped her to process and be a part of her dying. She said that she was not strong enough to do this, but after she had died, she went to a place where she saw the effect this had on Olivia and how her daughter had built the steel gate around her heart as a way of protecting her from love. Her mother had watched over Olivia and had been waiting for a time when she could help her daughter. She was so thankful for this time, and that her daughter could now be released of her pain so she could truly love again.

At the close of the session we grounded this mother's love into the cells of Olivia and suggested that she would be able to contact her mother and feel her love whenever she wanted or needed to. This session changed this young woman's life and she was able to fully embrace the relationship she desired.

I deeply love this work. To touch the soul of another like this is a great blessing. It has happened time and time again where the spirit of a deceased person has been hanging out and waiting for the opportunity to participate in the healing of their loved one here on earth. It seems that after this, the soul is free to move on.

A second example of this work comes from the opposite direction. Samuel was the youngest son of a family of four. Although a good kid, he didn't excel in sports like his older brother and could not compete with his two sisters for his father's attention. His mother was the one who gave him the most attention, but her own dysfunction and alcohol problem made this more of a liability than an advantage in his life.

Samuel's mother had not wanted a fourth child and was all too willing to let Samuel know that whenever she felt frustrated or when he would do something wrong. She blamed him for herself not being able to go back to school and live her dream. Of course Samuel was not the cause, but only a convenient scapegoat. His mother, possibly to relieve her guilt, would give Samuel special treats and give him attention that caused resentment amongst his siblings. This is the most difficult position for any child to be in, to depend upon a parent who goes from kind to abusive and back, often without reason. Samuel loved and hated his mother. Of course he stifled the hate because he needed her and eventually this long held emotion settled into cancer.

When Samuel came to me, the cancer had advanced and his prognosis was poor. He had been reading about how body, mind and spirit were all linked and wondered if his body had something to say to him. It certainly did! He was able to uncover feelings about his mother that were literally *eating him alive*. He cried and asked her how she could have been so cruel to him. During the session her response was to tell him that she had never been able to have her dreams and that she didn't know how to be a mother. Her own mother died when she was a young girl and she was left, the oldest of three children, with her alcoholic father to raise her siblings. Everyone came before her and that is what she learned. Samuel was still angry. *"That's no excuse!"* he shouted out, and then another presence came into the room. It was the spirit of his grandmother, whom he had never seen. Samuel didn't understand how he knew it was her, but he did. Her energy was filled with love and compassion, and he felt the comfort she brought. He then *saw,* in his mind's eye, the cycle in this family of abandonment and abuse that had been carried on for generations. Samuel knew that he was being called now to break this chain, but could he? After all, he was sick and hurting too. How could he let it go, and what, pretend it was now all OK?

As Samuel connected more with his grandmother's energy, his heart began to soften and he could see how the anger he had been holding for his mother was harming his body and not hers. He was able to grasp that she did love him and did the best she could during her physical life, and although that did not excuse how she behaved towards him, this knowledge along with the love he was taking in from his grandmother began to erode the anger that was fused so strongly in his cells that felt like a part of him. Samuel could see how he was perpetuating the history of his ancestors by holding onto the anger and blaming his mother for what he lacked in his life. It may look a little different, but he saw how it was exactly what his mother had done and how she lived her life. Grandmother told Samuel that his mother had not learned enough in the spirit world where she now was, and so she was not able to envelop him in love like his grandmother was. Grandmother went on to say that if Samuel could truly forgive his mother and rise vibrationaly above the anger, not only would he be, but he would help his mother as well. Breathing and allowing his grandmother to assist, Samuel was able to release the anger and bring peaceful energy into his body to fill all the spaces where the anger had been. His cancer went into remission. As to whether it was completely healed I do not know, but his soul found peace and healing for certain.

Born Again

"To take down the veil of lies and open your heart and mind to who you truly are. To experience Oneness with the Divine, and the joy of a child; that, is to be born again."

~ Linda Baker

Mary, Sam, Maria, George ..... so many clients have lied down on the healing grid bed for Spiritual Hypnotherapy sessions and have been, in my eyes, *reborn*. I have been midwife to these births, a sacred honor to be present for the re-birth of each client that has gone through this process. What does it mean to be reborn?

I had never thought about this or associated Alchemical/Spiritual Hypnotherapy work with being reborn, until I experienced my first rebirth. We had been working on inner childhood issues during our session, when Kim began to experience tightening within her body. As she cried and her body contracted, the waves coming and going, in such a way that it reminded me of the process of labor. I rubbed her back as she lay on her side going through the labor of her rebirth. It was amazing and beautiful to witness this process. By the end of her labor she had *delivered* a new self.

I guided her to take this baby to a crystal clear pond of the perfect depth and temperature. She held this precious being and walked into the crystal healing waters where she bathed this baby, washing away the old beliefs that had made her feel unworthy, dirty and bad. She had the baby drink of this natural healing water to purify it from within, cleansing and releasing toxins from the past and then, upon taking the baby out of the water, wrapped her in a soft, warm blanket and while holding this sweet child close to her heart, Kim 'd herself. She told the baby how sweet and beautiful told her that she was good and smart and was a child with creative ideas and unlimited potential. Kim told this baby-self everything she wished she had heard from her own parents, and when she was finished, she held a baby free of the old guilt, shame, fears and doubts that she had carried all these years. Kim was reborn.

As I've witnessed clients transform through this process, it is clear to me that re-birth, being reborn, or born again is a spiritual process that allows one to release the lies, old programming and any energy that has caused separation from God, or the Divine Source of all life, and brings us into a state of ONENESS with that Source Energy. In the state of rebirth, one's vibrations are lifted and one is filled with the light of love and divinity. The false veil of separation between the small self and the True Self is lifted. Once we have a glimpse of whom we truly are and feel the love the Divine has for us, it is impossible to slip completely back into our old way of thinking and being. Of course we may have been addicted to past programming and negativity and those old thoughts and beliefs may try to bring us back to the past, but through practicing the homework given at the conclusion of each session, and because of the vibrational shift in the cells, the True One will always prevail.

Section VI
Spiritual Post-Conception
Birth Control

"We're swimming through a river of change. We've spent the last decade standing on the river bank, rescuing women who are drowning. In the next decade, some of us have to go to the head of the river to keep women from falling in"

~ Gloria Steinam

The Process

∽

"Greater is she who acts from love, than she who acts from fear."
~ Simeon Ben Sleazar

For many years now I have been providing special sessions to women who find themselves pregnant when they do not wish to be. I call these sessions post-conception birth control or a *spiritual approach to abortion.* I believe that we are spirit and that we have come into the physical realm for learning and experience. If this is so, then why not communicate with the spirit of the unborn child and let it know that this is not right timing?

This approach enables the spirit of the unborn child to consciously participate in the abortion decision. It is a loving approach that seems to be tremendously healing. The basis for the spiritual abortion process comes from the belief that when you enter the physical realm as a baby, your body is small and needs to be taken care of, but your soul may be old and full of wisdom. If this is true for a baby then it is also true for the unborn child, the one just beginning to develop a physical body inside of the womb that holds it. We can communicate with this spirit just as we can with a loved one who has passed on. The spirit of an unborn child is filled with wisdom and always has a powerful lesson to share with the mother and father.

In 1991 I wrote an article entitled the *Spiritual Approach to Abortion* for the Seattle *New Times,* a metaphysical newspaper. I received numerous letters and telephone calls from women who read this article. Many women wanted to tell me their story of spontaneous abortions they had experienced. They told me how they had prayed, meditated, lit candles, chanted and than naturally miscarried.

As I heard and read these accounts a part of me awakened to the knowledge that this process was natural for women in times long past. I believe there was a time when women understood the power and the sacredness of their bodies, and were able to make conscious choices about when or when not give birth. That power was taken over by a male dominated society, but now this ancient wisdom of the Goddess is reawakening in women.

Alchemical/Spiritual Hypnotherapy makes it possible for the mother to connect with the spirit of the unborn child, so that together, they can agree upon a natural miscarriage. Of the women I have worked with, several have naturally miscarried shortly after their sessions while others have needed to have clinical abortions. When women have clinical abortions scheduled just following their session and they follow through with the abortion, it is impossible to know whether or not the process would have occurred naturally. My belief is that as more women become aware of this option, it will become easier for them to have natural abortions, and that it will become easier for women to consciously choose when to become pregnant.

When I first began doing this work I felt that if the miscarriage did not happen naturally, the process did not work. I no longer feel that way. I now understand that everyone woman has her own process to go through, and sometimes that process includes a clinical abortion. Whether or not miscarriage occurs as a result of this process, the process is always powerful and contains wisdom and emotional healing from guilt, fear, grief, or whatever emotions the woman carries.

Women from all over the country have called me to ask who in their area is doing this spiritual post conception birth control work. Since I was unaware of others doing this, I would explain the process over the telephone and wish them well. After having received several return calls from these women and finding that some were able to naturally miscarry, I decided to make an audiotape of the process to be used by those wishing to abort as well as those wishing to heal from past abortion or miscarriage.

One Christian woman became pregnant out of wedlock requested the tape because her religion does not permit abortion. She and her boyfriend said that they would listen to it and leave the results to God.

The woman called me two weeks later with the news that after she and her boyfriend listened to the tape several times, she miscarried. They both expressed great thinks to me and felt relieved that God had given them their wish. For more information on this tape, please see the appendix at the end of this book.

From a practical standpoint, as anyone in the business world knows, responsibility must accompany authority in order for a system to be effective. Although women hold the responsibility for childbearing, in many cultures it has been the men who take power or assume authority in this arena. We don't have to look far back into history before we see such prevailing views as *barefoot and pregnant* and *a woman's place is in the home.* Even popular songs from the sixties encourage young girls to *"Wear your hair just for him and do the things he likes to do."* Generally speaking, men took, and still take, pride in getting their wives pregnant, especially when a son is involved. In some cultures, the more children, especially male children a man fathers, the more manly he is considered to be. Women often had to take responsibility for their pregnancies through birth control, but even birth control was or is not allowed by certain major religions. I wonder if it because men cannot bear children themselves, that some fear women's power, and thus historically have striven to make it appear as if they are the ones in control? I want to stress here that in no way do I include all men in this statement. Many men share in the responsibilities of conception and caring for a child as well as honor and support women's rights, while there are women who are against a woman's right to choose.

Spiritual Hypnotherapy is extremely valuable for both post-conception birth control and healing from miscarriage. The process is valuable for both women and men. Although the mother carries the child, there is learning for the father as well, and sometimes the spirit of the fetus is even more connected to the father than to the mother. When an abortion or miscarriage takes place and there no spiritual healing involved, and so such feelings as grief, guilt, anger, and fear may become stuck in the body. In a woman, these often center in the reproductive organs. Naturopathic physicians have told me that many women who have ovarian cancer, cysts, fibroid tumors, abnormal bleeding and other *female problems* have experienced an abortion or miscarriage at sometime in their lives. In our modern medical environment a hysterectomy is often offered as the cure.

The womb is the center of the feminine body. It is the birthing center of creativity, but the beauty of this is little recognized in our society. In this country, women commonly hear, *"You're not going to have any more children"* or, *"You're past the childbearing age, so let's do a hysterectomy."* What message does this give to a woman? I think that the message that a woman receives is that her creative worth, (the womb being the center of creativity) is defined by bearing children. I bring attention to this because claiming personal power and creativity has been the major issue with several of my clients. Pregnancy fills the womb, the baby is the creation and the pay-off is safety. Society claims it acceptable for a woman to focus on birth and babies, and so childbearing can be a good camouflage for those who are afraid to look into themselves and face the fears, doubts and inadequacies that keep their expression of personal creative force at a distance. Of course, these women are not aware that they are masking something until they take that journey within the self.

Men also hold unresolved feelings in their bodies. Men who have been partners in abortion/miscarriage have suggested to me that the energy they hold may concentrate in the third chakra, the center of power. In the case of a miscarriage, a man might feel that he was not powerful, potent, or manly enough to save the baby. In abortion, it might be that the man feels that he did something wrong, that it was his fault and he doesn't deserve to have what he wants. I'm sure that there are many other possible beliefs or feelings. If you are a man who has had an experience with miscarriage or abortion, take a moment to close your eyes and imagine the experience, feel your feelings around this issue and notice where they live in your body.

Spiritual Hypnotherapy allows the woman to go deep within the womb so that she can explore the core beliefs and judgments that she holds, and that may have been held by women throughout the fabric of time, past and present. Some common beliefs held by women are: the need to nurture others and put themselves last; that they must have children to be worthwhile; a need for a man to take care of them and that they are the weaker sex and are not in control of their bodies. Many women who perceive themselves to be independent, strong, and freethinking have been appalled to find such beliefs lurking in their innermost psyche. It is amazing to see how core beliefs that we are consciously unaware of, or thought we had let go of, determine what we attract into our lives. Through the Spiritual Hypnotherapy process, these hidden elements come to the surface where they can be healed and released.

With every spiritual abortion session, the child's spirit brings a message of learning to the mother and father, and in many instances, this message involves the importance of nurturing and caring for one's own inner child. Women who are questioning whether or not to have a child can contact and support their child within. This liberates them from the need to have an outer child and allows them the freedom to make a healthy choice about pregnancy.

I believe that it would be good for every person who wants a child to do inner-child work prior to conception. One of the most common issues between parents and children is the desire of the parent to control the child and mold the child into what the parent wants. When the child, who desires to find a healthy, independent identity, rebels, the pain and separation that result are often blamed on the child. To avoid this the child may instead become the *good* child and live his/her life trying to please the parent rather then fully becoming his/her own person. If a parent is not nurturing his/her own inner child, the outer child becomes a substitute and focal point for the parent. In place of a functional, supportive parent who encourages the child to individuate, the dysfunctional parent controls, either subtly or overtly, to have their own needs met and fulfilled by the child.

When a woman chooses to do a spiritual post conception birth control session prior to a clinical abortion, she is often able to learn the lesson from the pregnancy, as well as speak directly to the spirit of the child. Some of the most common lessons the spirit comes to teach are about healing the inner child, bringing forth creative energy, empowering the self, healing relationship issues and healing from past abortions or miscarriages so that the mother may choose a healthy new pregnancy. Sometimes the connection between the woman and the unborn child runs very deep and the mother experiences feelings of great love and pain in letting go. It is important to remember that pain does not equal bad or wrong. A right choice in our lives can bring feelings of loss, grief or loneliness and still be the right choice for us. For example, leaving an abusive relationship may bring up many painful feelings and still be the best, healthy choice to make.

The love Spirit has for us is so strong that I have had many clients burst into tears when they feel this energy. It is the purest love they have ever felt, with no demand, no desire and no judgment involved, they experience pure love. Over and over I have been witness to how loving and forgiving Spirit is.

One concern that has been expressed to me is the fear that action we take to prevent a spirit from taking on a physical body denies life to that spirit. Spirit is energy and can never be denied life or given life, because spirit is life, and God/Divine Energy gives that life. In my experience, there are times when the spirit has contracted to become physical to be of assistance to a parent, but would rather not be in physical body. Sometimes in a session a spirit will *say "I am so glad that you can get the message this way so I don't have to take a body!"* To think that our physical plane is desired by all, and is the ultimate experience, may be a bit presumptuous. Through the work that I have done, I have felt and seen how loving and forgiving spirit is, how connected the physical and spiritual world are, and how important it is for each one of us to honor our highest truth.

I have been asked if there are times when a spirit does not agree to leave. The answer is yes, this does happen, but only with women who have issues of not living in their power and always wanting to please others. I remember three cases when the spirit came forth with, *"No, I will not go."* Each of these times the client had to work on being willing to make the right choice for her. Each time when the woman took her power and demanded *"This is my body. The timing is not right and you must leave."* the spirit was joyful and said this was the lesson to be learned.

Just because spirit is spirit does not mean it is experiencing an enlightened state of being. When a spirit has been aborted without prior communication it may remain attached to the mother's energy field in a confused, frightened, or angry state. This occurred for one of my clients who became pregnant, but had a feeling like something was wrong. She shared with me that she had an abortion three years earlier and was worried that this might affect the child she was now

144

carrying. When she entered into a deep state of stillness during the session, she suddenly became afraid and said, *"There's something out here and I'm afraid it's going to hurt my child!"* I could feel the energy in my body as well, and I could see the fear in her. When I asked if she knew who it was, she immediately got that it was the spirit of the child she had aborted. It was a male energy and he was very angry that this little girl child was in the womb. He said, *"I was supposed to be the one!"* The client became even more fearful when she heard this. I asked if there were any guides that could come to care for this one and immediately angels came and surrounded him with love. His energy softened, and as he began to move away with the angels, he also began to forget her. The client saw that he would be born to someone else and would enter into this world again in a healthier state of being. She felt at peace with her decision of abortion and was able to carry on with her pregnancy with a positive energy.

When I speak of this alternative to clinical abortion, some people become concerned that helping women to awaken to this process will encourage people to be reckless with preventing pregnancy because they can just talk to the spirit and tell it to go. I don't think that this is likely. Doing this work takes commitment to self-healing. It is an inner process that requires courage and the willingness to explore individual truth. It is a spiritual process and not a simple command ordering spirit to leave. This work does not encourage abortion, but allows spiritual healing for the mother, father, and spirit, when abortion is the choice. I truly believe that as women become more aware of spirit and inner healing work, they will communicate more easily with their bodies and that this consciousness will result in fewer unwanted pregnancies.

I have spoken mainly of the mother with regard to this work that is who generally comes to do these sessions, but I have worked with both parents together and I have worked solely with the father. At these times I have witnessed men do wonderful work by communicating with the child they had lost, or were soon to lose through abortion. One of the lessons that frequently comes up for men is the fear of commitment. A spirit child once told her grieving father, *"When you can clearly commit to fathering a child you shall have one."* Other lessons that come up for men are those of the wounded inner child and relationship issues.

I have selected the following stories to illustrate this Spiritual Post-Conception Birth Control process. I hope these stories give you greater insight as to how spirit makes itself known, and how a spirit may contract to assist a woman, or man, in achieving greater consciousness and healing.

Andrea

"The bravest are the tenderest. The loving are the daring."
~ Henry Wadsworth Longfellow

Andrea was a pretty young woman who came to me because she wasn't sure that she wanted the child she was carrying, and was considering a medical abortion. She and the father had been together for nearly two years and, although he was looking forward to a family, now was not the time. They wanted to plan a wedding and be married before they took this next step. Andrea told me that she and the father had a very good relationship; she felt he would make an excellent father, and he was willing to step up their plans, but she was the problem. She felt that she didn't deserve to have a child and that she would be inadequate as a mother.

As we spoke, Andrea confided that she had already had two abortions, one at age sixteen and another at nineteen. As a result, she was afraid this baby would not be born healthy. She was afraid that her body had been damaged and that she would be punished for having had the abortions. I told Andrea about how other women had connected with the spirits of those who were aborted or miscarried and asked her if she would be willing to try to access these souls. Although she was afraid, she wanted to do the work and contact these beings.

Both of the spirits were female in energy. They came to Andrea quickly, and she felt their presence as well as their love. They told her that they loved her and forgave her but that she needed to forgive herself. Andrea cried and said that she did not know how, or even if she could do this. First, I had her call forth her sixteen-year-old self, who was shy and scared. I asked the present Andrea to look into the eyes of the sixteen-year-old Andrea, but she didn't want to because she felt only anger for this young girl. Finally she was able to connect with this self and feel her pain. She began to understand how this young girl was only looking for love, and as her home life was abusive, she was willing to look anywhere. A young man had spoken the words she longed to hear, *"I love you,"* but left her as soon as she told him she was pregnant. Andrea was left with feelings of shame and guilt and the feeling that her only choice was to have an abortion. Although her parents supported this decision, they made certain that she knew that they disapproved of her actions. Andrea wept as she remembered her pain and finally was able to hold her sixteen-year-old self and tell her that she loved her and that she forgave her.

Meeting herself at nineteen was easier because she had already experienced the first healing. The situations were similar, and Andrea forgave this young woman as well. As all three Andreas embraced and held hands, the present-day Andrea felt a freedom and inner love that she had not known before. The spirits of her unborn children told Andrea that they had been waiting for her to recognize them so that she could receive their love and, most importantly, forgive herself. They said that this new baby was also a girl, and that Andrea would make a fine mother, but that it was *very* important that she forgive herself first. They were the ones that Andrea was feeling when she felt she would not make a good mother. They wanted her to do this healing. They told her that the spirit of this baby would feel the energy shift with this forgiveness and self-love. This would energetically shift the baby's consciousness as well and she would be happier for it. Andrea felt a great sense of relief, self-forgiveness, and self-love. She felt her desire to have this child. Today she is a happy mother who loves her little daughter very much.

In this story, we see how there was a contract with the spirits of the first two pregnancies. They agreed to stay with Andrea until the time she was able to speak with them and learn this lesson of self-love and forgiveness. After this was completed, the spirits were free to move into the light of the spirit realm.

Molly

"I restore myself when I'm alone."
~ Marilyn Monroe

"You cannot be lonely if you like the person you're alone with."
~ Wayne Dyer

Molly had married and raised three children, and now at the age of forty she was pregnant again, but neither she nor her husband wanted another child. They were using birth control and felt somewhat betrayed to find themselves in this situation. Although Molly logically agreed that it was not in their family's best interest to have another child, she also felt a relief in being pregnant. In the past, Molly had somehow always ensured that at least one of her children or her husband was around her at all times, and now her youngest was turning eighteen and leaving for college, she would be alone while her husband was off on business trips. If ever a situation arose in which no one in her family was present, she would arrange to go out shopping or visit a friend, as she just didn't do well by herself. Now that her last child was ready to move out and her husband's trips were more frequent, Molly was experiencing anxiety attacks at even the thought of being alone. Being pregnant, and the thought of having another child at home with her, helped ease these feelings. Yet when she looked logically at her life, it did not make sense to have another child. Molly had heard of the spiritual post-conception work and decided to find out more about it. She also hoped this work would help her overcome her fear of being alone.

As Molly and I discussed her history, we could not find any conscious memory that seemed connected to her fear of being alone. Because of her religious upbringing, Molly did not believe in past lives, and so we began the session with the intent of regressing to an unconscious childhood experience related to the fear. We also agreed to see in what other ways this pregnancy might be connected to her fear, and if the spirit had any information for her about this.

During the last phase of Spiritual Hypnosis trance induction, Molly found herself in a log cabin. When asked what she was wearing, she replied, *"A kind of buckskin dress and bare feet."* Although I suspected that this was a past life memory, I did not say anything and proceeded to help Molly connect more deeply with this image. She said that she felt about four years old and lived in the log cabin with her parents and grandmother. Her family was part of a small settlement with nothing but trees and new fields surrounding it. She witnessed an attack by a band of natives and watched her grandmother die from an arrow in her chest, and in the chaos of the attack, Molly's parents directed her to hide in a type of root cellar until they could come for her. There, by herself, this little girl began to feel the same overwhelming terror that Molly experienced in her present-day form whenever she was alone.

To help Molly detach from the pain and fear of being there, I instructed her to rise above the scene and watch it happening from above. Molly saw that the settlement was destroyed and her parents killed. She also saw that the terrified little girl remained in hiding and died waiting for her parents to return. Molly realized that her little girl self had died with a deep fear of being left alone. I then took Molly back to that time so that she could *rerun* this scenario and change it. In this new scene everything happened as it had before, except when the attack was over a kind, angel-like, woman came into the root cellar, took the little girl in her arms and comforted her. Then the woman gently lifted the little girl away to another life.

The session was powerful and Molly experienced a great deal of emotional release. She was now able to go into a place of deep peace and meet with the spirit of the fetus. The message for her was that this pregnancy was meant to bring her to the place where she would have to deal with her fear of being alone. It was important for her to be free of this energy so that she could have the liberty to live life for herself. The spirit said that it did not wish to be born and had come for the purpose of helping her become conscious. It told her that if she had an abortion without doing this work, her process would have been much more difficult, and that maybe she never would have learned the lesson, but only added guilt to her already existing fear.

After our session, Molly became concerned because she was uncomfortable with having what could be interpreted as a past life experience. We talked about how her experience could instead be viewed as a metaphor, or story symbolizing the trauma that the child within her experienced when left alone. This was easier for her to relate to. With past life work, it is not the belief system but the healing that is important. The experiences that surface can be viewed as archetypal, past life or genetic, and I use whichever lens the client is comfortable with.

In the following weeks, Molly experienced dramatic improvement. Molly had come to view the little girl in the session as symbolic of her own present-life inner child who needed to be mothered and made to feel safe. She did her *homework,* which entailed spending time each day, nurturing, talking with, and creating a safe place for the abandoned little girl she had encountered in her session. Molly had done this for her own children, now it was time for her to do this for herself. As she did, her fears of being alone dissipated. Molly did proceed to have a clinical abortion, which went well for her. She felt at peace with her decision and healed quickly. Her big test came two weeks after the abortion when her husband was called out of town for a two-day meeting. In the past, Molly would have panicked and made frantic arrangements to fill her days, but now, though she did arrange a visit with a friend, she was able to focus on fun at-home activities that she could do by herself, and she discovered that she actually could enjoy and discover an inner calmness when she was alone.

The Treasure

"Give a little love to a child, (the child within – author's note) *and you get a great deal back."*

~ John Ruskin

Anne first came to see me when she was about six weeks pregnant and quite unhappy. She had arranged to leave an unhealthy relationship only to discover she was pregnant. None of the alternatives she considered, including staying with her current partner and *"making the best of it,"* becoming a single mother, or having an abortion, felt right to her. After reading about the Spiritual Post-Conception work, she immediately contacted me and scheduled an appointment.

Anne and I began our first session with the usual methods of attaining deep awareness and relaxation. Anne soon found herself opening a large wooden door and stepping into a many-sided room with large windows that allowed sunlight to stream inside. Piles of soft, brightly colored cushions scattered about the room gave it a friendly and inviting atmosphere, and as Anne moved around noticing the colors, she became aware of a non-physical light presence that appeared to be feminine in nature. This Being was free-floating, as it had not yet settled into physical existence. Anne was attracted to the softness of this presence and asked, *"Are you the spirit child within me?"* The affirmative answer was not actually spoken, but Anne felt it through her inner knowing. Anne explained why she was here and how she needed to leave the unhealthy relationship with her partner. She explained that having a child now would serve no one involved, but that she would gladly invite the spirit child in at another time when she was in the kind of relationship she wanted, with a man who would make a loving father.

The spirit child seemed to under-stand and was happy to postpone physical incarnation. The spirit child then requested that Anne call forth her own inner child. Anne did this and looked on as a quiet, shy little girl stepped into the room. After some coaxing the little girl said that she was afraid that Anne, who had minimal contact with her now, would completely abandon her if she had a baby. The spirit child spoke saying, *"You need to become acquainted with this little child, to nurture her and to play with her because when I return I do not want to take her place."* Anne heard these words and then sat down with little Anne on a pile of pillows so that she and this little inner child could talk. Little Anne said that she wanted to wear pretty dresses and to go to the park and play on the swings. She also wanted to go for walks by the water, ride her bicycle, and have a soft cuddly teddy bear to hold. Adult Anne, with tears in her eyes, listened to and held her inner child. She told her that not only would she take care of her and do these things, but also assured her that she would never leave her, no matter how many babies she had. Little Anne, although happy, was somewhat skeptical of this. Anne felt her concern and asked how they could keep in contact. Little Anne said that she was always available as part of Anne's inner wisdom and that all Anne needed to do was to close her eyes and return to this room.

As Anne prepared to leave this room, the spirit child reassured Anne that she had already left the physical body. Anne then embraced her own inner child, aware that she had rediscovered a precious treasure. She had Little Anne melt into her heart where she would be safe, remembered, and surrounded with love.

As Anne opened the door to leave the room she discovered a long corridor. There was a sign with arrows pointing: *This way to the uterus* and one pointing: *This way to the brain*. Anne chose to visit the uterus first. At the end of the hall she entered the uterus through a heavy, soft, thick, red velvet curtain. She found herself standing in a warm, dark room with red walls. As she lit a lantern she noticed a small man who then asked her why she was there. Anne explained to him her desire to release the pregnancy and that the spirit child had already receded from the fetus. The man agreed to help. She also wanted to see the fetus and asked the man if he would show it to her. He led her deeper into the room, taking her to the place where the physical form of the spirit child rested. Anne described it as small, bean shaped and lifeless. Anne watched as the little man began to separate it from the uterine wall and as he did this, she asked what else needed to be done. The little man showed her the mucous plug and said he could not remove it until he had help. Anne called upon her inner guide who came forth, ready to help, but not until Anne was back home where she felt safe and supported. The little man agreed to wait and said that he would do all of the cleansing in preparation for the removal of this plug. Anne thanked him for his help and with her guidance left the uterus to go visit the brain.

In the brain a tall woman, who informed her that she already knew what had transpired between Anne and the spirit child, greeted Anne and told her that appropriate adjustments her had already been made. The woman advised Anne to check her breasts often throughout the miscarriage process, to send love to her heart, drink as much water as she could and get plenty of rest. Anne asked the woman if she could do something so that there wouldn't be any pain with this process. The woman assured Anne that she would assist in alleviating the pain.

Anne felt that she would miscarry at the time of her normal menstrual cycle and imagined the desired outcome with Future Pacing. (Future pacing is a technique where the hypnotherapist suggests that the client imagine a time in the future. The purpose is to see how the client responds to the session.) In this case Anne imagined the time of her next menstrual cycle. When she did this she felt herself having the miscarriage. She returned home, and during the next week, which was the time of her normal menstrual period, she miscarried easily and with little discomfort.

Several years have passed and Anne is now married to a wonderful man whom she loves. Together they have a sweet little daughter. Is this the same soul that Anne met in the session? It well could be.

In Anne's session, I find it is interesting that a little man was the caretaker of the uterus and a woman the caretaker of the brain. In most sessions I have done it is exactly the opposite. One of the most powerful aspects of this work is that it does not follow any formula.

It is always guided by spirit and that is what allows transformation to occur. Also, please note that this visit to the uterus and the brain is a part of every Spiritual Post-Conception Birth Control session, even if it was not included in the story.

The Child in the Garden

~

"A small boy looked at a star and began to weep. The star said, 'Boy, why are you weeping?' And the boy said, 'You are so far away I will never be able to touch you.' And the star answered, 'Boy, if I were not already in your heart, you would not be able to see me."

~ John Magliola

Angie was pregnant for the third time in a six-month period. She had miscarried with her first pregnancy and had a clinical abortion with the second. She came to me for help in connecting with the spirit child so that she could learn from this experience.

After the trance induction, Angie stepped through a beautiful blue door into a lush garden full of tall, brightly colored flowers and softly singing birds. She started walking towards an ornately carved stone fountain at the garden's center, and as she approached, she could hear the sound of water as it cascaded into the fountain's stone basin. Here a little girl was standing quietly by the fountain's edge, and Angie knew immediately that she was the spirit child. Angie started to cry as she knelt down beside this little one and told her how sorry she was that she did not want her in her life at this time. The spirit child told Angie, *"I know all about you. I know you do not wish a child, but I wanted to come anyway to see what would happen."* Angie asked why she had chosen her, and the little girl answered, *"Because you are so sweet and you have such a spiritual connection to life. I want a mother who is that way. I like you so much and want to stay with you."*

Angie responded by telling the little girl how much she loved her, but that she could not be her mother as did not wish to have a child at this time. Angie then asked if this being had come to her before. *"Yes"* answered the spirit child, and told her that she had been present at one other time. Angie told the spirit child that she deserved to find a mother who was willing to bring her forth into the physical world. The little girl sadly acknowledged that this was true and that she would have to go from this place. She also let Angie know how much she was enjoying this contact with her. Angie took a moment to hold her in her arms. She felt that this Being was a part of her in a very special way and that they were both gifts to each other. While held in Angie's arms, the spirit child said that she was afraid that Angie would focus upon the loss rather than remember the loving communication they had shared. Angie thanked the little girl and said that she would do her best to focus on what was gained from this rather than on what was lost. The spirit child then receded, and the garden became quiet and still.

Angie left the garden and proceeded along a pathway to the uterus. She stepped through a pink triangular door into a cylindrically shaped cave with soft pink walls. She looked up and noticed the caretaker was a non-physical energy floating near the top of the cave. Angie addressed her as *Womb Mother*. This being was aware of all that had happened, and informed Angie that she had already begun to cleanse the uterine lining from the walls. Angie thanked her for the care and support and asked if Womb Mother would now be willing to help with releasing all the tissue. Womb Mother floated down from the top of the cave and slowly took human form. Angie could feel Womb Mother's compassion as they embraced. Womb Mother said that she would need assistance with the overall process and wanted Angie to be a part of it. *"Angie,"* she said, *"it is important for you to remember that your body is an important part of yourself and that it really does desire to work with you. Your body is your friend."*

Angie asked about the mucous plug and Womb Mother replied that she would need Angie's help to release it. They both stepped over and leaned against it. Angie enjoyed working with her body in this way and started to feel the energy move, she asked how she could stay open to communication with Womb Mother. *"My dear one,"* replied Womb Mother, *"just bring to your mind an image of the two of us embracing."*

After visiting the uterus, Angie stepped out of the cave and found herself on another path where she encountered a plain white door with the words HORMONE CONTROL written on the outside. She pushed open the door and entered a dimly lit lavender colored padded room. A scientist in a white lab coat was in charge here, and so engrossed in her work that she did not notice the visitor until Angie tapped her lightly on the shoulder. The scientist turned, smiled, and extended a hand to greet her. Angie commented upon the efficient job that she was doing, and the scientist replied that she liked her job very much and enjoyed making things run smoothly. After she was informed about the meetings with both the spirit child and Womb Mother, the scientist knew that the work she had been doing to prepare the body for this pregnancy was no longer necessary. Angie asked if the scientist would be willing to reverse the process and return her body back to its non-pregnant state. *"Yes, I accept your situation and do not foresee any problem,"* the scientist replied. *"I could not have helped you if you had not told me of your situation and asked for assistance. Now that I have this information I am able to change it over at the control center. What I will do will help your body return to its regular and normal cycles."* They both entered a room where there were multicolored dials and switches. The scientist adjusted the progesterone and estrogen levers, informing Angie that she would check hourly to make certain the hormones were at the proper pre-pregnancy levels. The scientist then asked Angie if she had spoken with her hypothalamus gland. Angie replied that she had not, so the scientist pointed the way to another door with the sign HYPOTHALAMUS on it.

Angie knocked on the hypothalamus door and then entered. It was a dimly lit and oddly shaped room with five sides and a very low ceiling. She walked to the front of the room where the light was better and noticed a short person sitting in a chair. This person was an energetic and ageless being, possessing qualities of both youth and old age. The person motioned for Angie to have a seat. This guide greeted Angie and then said, *"It is good that you have come to see me to check your overall state of health."* Angie liked and trusted this being. The guide explained to her that a fluid excreted here served as a chemical communicant throughout the body. The guide further explained how, because of inner stress, the impulses had not been steady enough so the overall health of the body had become weak and this caused Angie to feel out of sync with herself and her surrounding environment. *"Regulation of these impulses gives a feeling of oneness within and without,"* the guide told Angie. The guide also told Angie that her help was needed for the hypothalamus to work properly. *"I want you to feel your whole body working together. It's like the feeling you have when you are in meditation posture. Your serenity and sense of oneness will help me to regulate this."* Angie then spent several minutes in silence learning from her guide. When she again spoke, she told me that she felt a very clear communication with this part of herself and that she could easily contact this guide during meditation so that they could work together.

Both Angie and I felt positive after her session. We both believed that there would be no difficulty in releasing the unneeded tissue. However, three days later she called to tell me that she was still having morning sickness. The condition continued for another three days so we decided to meet for a second session.

Once more Angie entered into that deep state of relaxation where she met with the hormone control scientist. This time the scientist was waiting for Angie. *"You have been doing a good job of being in touch with your body, however the symptoms of pregnancy remain because you are stuck back in the moment when you met the spirit child in the garden. Every time I shift the hormone levels, you cause them to shift back to pregnancy levels. You are stopping this process because you want to feel what it is to be a child again."* Angie acknowledged that when she met the little girl she had felt great warmth in her heart and wanted to be like her. The scientist gently said, *"What you need to do is to go and meet your inner child, she is that part of you who is innocent and sweet and is always with you and available to you. You need not be pregnant to be with her and feel her love. She is here waiting to meet you, may I invite her in now?"*

Angie felt a little nervous, but was willing to meet her inner child. The door opened and Little Angie appeared dressed in jeans with a white T-shirt with sandals on her feet and pink ribbons in her hair.

Angie quickly walked over and picked her up. *"She is the essence of me and I feel sad because I don't know how to be more like her. She is the part of me that likes to play and that feels light and happy, never worried or concerned. How can I have you more in my life? I love you very much!"* Little Angie replied, *"It is not a problem for me to be part of your life. You are human and I am part of being human. I want you to play with me and hold me."*

Angie continued to speak with her inner child and together they went to an inner playground where they could run, swing, slide and just be with each other in the sunshine. Angie was taking the first steps in reclaiming her playful, sweet, and innocent nature. Little Angie reminded her of childhood feelings long forgotten. I had Angie imagine having this child with her in her present day life at work, at home alone and with her partner. When it was time to end the session Angie brought this inner child fully into her being by allowing her to melt into her heart center. She promised to spend time with this little one every day, to listen to her and make her an active part of her life. While Angie was bonding with her inner child, I sensed the presence of the spirit child and her delight that Angie had returned to be with her own inner child. This spirit child had given Angie a wonderful gift.

The scientist was pleased with this communication; however, Angie confided to her that although she felt a strong connection with her inner child, she was still feeling some doubt about the process working. The scientist understood and told Angie that this was a process of learning about herself and her needs, and that at this very moment while they were speaking her body was adjusting back to normal. Angie asked if there was a sign her body could give her so that she would feel more confident that the process was successful? At this moment Angie experienced a tingling sensation in her legs and warmth in her lower back. The scientist confirmed that these were signs that the body was indeed returning to its natural non-pregnant state. She recommended that Angie play with her inner child over the next few days to deepen the bond between them, and that this would help her body complete the process. We finished the session by future-pacing both this bonding and the miscarriage process. Everything checked out as completed at this time.

Angie reported several days later that she noticed a new lightness in her life and realized that this child part of her allowed her to give and receive love more easily. She also informed me that she had made the choice to have a clinical abortion. Her body had not yet started to release the tissue on it's own, and even though the feeling of the spirit child wishing to incarnate was no longer present, she decided that it was time to take this more traditional route. After the abortion, she told me that because of the traumatic experience of her first abortion she had been terrified that she might have to face that again, however, because of her work we had done, this abortion was an entirely different experience. Instead of feeling overwhelmed by fear and guilt, she moved through this second abortion feeling empowered, peaceful, and certain of her choice.

In many cases this work leads to a natural abortion and a clinical abortion is not needed. However, it appears that in some cases a clinical abortion is necessary for personal growth.

Section VII
In Conclusion

*"Sun and Moon and your own heart
speak always of that which abides.
In solitude and stillness Know that the journey
begins and ends with the self"*

~ Ralph Blum

Is It Real?

"The things we see," Pistorius said softly, "are the same things that are within us. There is no reality except the one contained within us. That is why so many people live such unreal lives. They take the images outside them for reality and never allow the world within to assert itself."

~ Herman Hesse, Demian

Now that you have read these stories and my theories concerning them, the skeptic in you might ask, *"Is any of this real?"* To answer that question let's take a moment to look at what the word *real* means.

In the *New Merriam-Webster Dictionary*, third edition, **real** is defined as:

1. fact, actually being or existent
2. not artificial: genuine.

In *Webster's New 20th Century Unabridged Dictionary,* **real** is defined as:
1. Actually being or existing, not fictitious or imaginary; as a description of *real* life.
2. True, genuine; not counterfeit, or fictitious.
3. *Real* presence: in various churches the actual presence of the body and blood of Christ in the Eucharist, or the conversion of the substance of the bread and wine into the real body and blood of Christ.

Even the dictionary contains definitions of *real* that one may or may not agree with. Who is to define what *real* life might be or what *real* honor or presence is? Most of us can agree on our experience of physical reality, such as the realness of a chair we are sitting on or the table holding our dinner, but outside of the obvious, physical realm we have disagreement.

A friend of mine lost her mother several years ago. She had gone for her usual weekly visit and found her mother lying dead upon the floor. The memory of this experience caused her great discomfort, sadness, and even depression until her mother *visited* her several weeks later and told her to stop worrying. Her mother said that she was very happy where she was and would be there to greet my friend when it was her time to come. Was this a real visitation, or only a figment of my friend's imagination? I cannot say. What I do know is that my friend had never before had such an experience, was not looking for such an experience and that after this experience she was her old self. The deep sadness and uncomfortable memories were gone.

When I address the topic of past lives in classes, students often want to know if they are really real. I reply that I believe they are real, and that is all I can say. I can only talk about my experiences and beliefs. As a group we then discuss our experiences, beliefs, and the alternative possibilities. If I were teaching in another culture, India for example, where most people take past lives and reincarnation for granted, I would expect less questions about this. Part of what we believe has to do with what we were taught to believe as children, neither good nor bad, right or wrong; its just how it is.

You may have heard the term the *collective unconscious*. This term refers to the idea that we are all connected with each other and with every living thing on the planet. Once, at a lecture, I heard Deepak Chopra say that as we breathe, we breathe out cells of our liver, lungs, heart and other organs and breathe in cells from others around us. Because we have always done this, says Chopra, all of us contain a number of cells from Jesus, Buddha, and countless others throughout time. Through our collective unconscious we can connect with everyone who lives and has lived before us, and during a state of meditation we can access knowledge from throughout the ages.

From this point of view we could say that past life memories are not personal, but rather those of a greater consciousness accessed via cellular memory. Thus, the experiences held in our bodies are not necessarily ours in a personal sense.

The collective unconscious explains the *"I was a famous person in my past life"* syndrome. Numerous people have proclaimed to me that they were Saint Joan of Arc, Cleopatra, Napoleon, Mary Magdalene, Michelangelo, or some other well-known personality. I have known several people who have claimed to have been the same historical figure. How could this be? It may be that their present life feels a bit mundane, they want to impress others, bolster their own ego, or use it to excuse why they haven't developed creative potential in this life. Of course, it could be also that there is truth in what those people claim. A great part of their spirits may be connected to one of these personalities, and therefore they can more easily draw upon memories or resources from these persons than others can.

In addition to the collective unconscious and past life theories, there is the theory that time is not linear and that past, present, and future are all happening at once. I find this theory fascinating and as plausible as any but my mind hasn't been able to quite grasp it. If you are interested in exploring this further, I recommend Richard Bach's book *One*. This book provides an enjoyable, well-crafted portrayal of the subject.

Then there is the heaven and hell perspective, atheism, and other theories that do not support the notion of past lives. With these belief systems, all we have is this one time to be in the physical body, and then we die. What happens next? It depends on which school of thought you come from. For some it is nothing, there is no soul and the body returns to dust - the end. For others it means the soul is freed and, depending upon how good or bad you were, you go happily to be with God, suffer eternally in hell, or get caught somewhere in between.

Maybe what we believe helps determine what our reality is. So are past lives real? Only you can answer that for yourself based upon your own experiences. From my personal experiences and from sessions I have witnessed, I without doubt, believe spirit does continue lifetime after lifetime, that we incarnate for a purpose, and that we connect with other souls who are part of our growth and learning in the same way that we are for theirs.

Sometimes a belief is held so strongly that it is accepted as truth without ever being challenged. For example, many years ago, I had the belief that it was impossible to walk over a bed of red-hot coals without getting burnt. This appeared to be a solid truth, until the first time I walked across a fire without getting burnt. This shattered my previous reality, and I experienced a huge release of emotion as something in my brain shifted. I wondered, *"What other limiting beliefs do I accept as absolute truth?"* I led firewalks for many years so that others could experience the teaching of the fire, move through limitations and question their beliefs.

Throughout the pages of this book we see that the circumstances of our lives are not about a God who punishes or rewards us for the actions that *we* judge to be good or bad, instead, every choice we make holds an opportunity for our soul's personal growth. Maybe hell is only a pattern of guilt, judgment and suffering that is repeated lifetime after lifetime and heaven is the freedom from this pattern.

God, Great Spirit, Divine Energy, is a loving energy that supports our growth and our desires to heal, love and live in accordance with our true nature. Through the Alchemical/ Spiritual work I have watched myself, students and clients release old, unwanted patterns, grow in consciousness and self-love and live in greater spiritual harmony with God, Goddess and all that is.

"From miracles you were made and to mystery you shall return."
~ an Ancient Mystic

The Crystal Healing Room

Since I have mentioned the Crystal Healing Room, where I do my work, I thought I would share a little about that room. In the photo with the grid bed, you can see the Vogel Crystal lights above the bed.

These crystals have lights, colored for the seven major chakras, behind them so that the color can be infused into the body for energy and healing. The word *crystal* comes from the Greek word *krystalios*, meaning frozen light. The crystal contains information and can also be programmed with intention to affect healing.

The three Vogel Crystals in the picture are used to help release stuck energy from the body. Of course, energy can be released without the use of the crystals, but I find that when I use them, they quicken the process. The crystals have served as a powerful catalyst for the rebirth sessions I have facilitated.

To explain the Vogel Crystals, I will tell you about Marcel Vogel. During a near-death experience Marcel, a very talented research scientist for IBM, had when he was a child, he experienced a light and sense of well-being so profound it changed his life. He had a

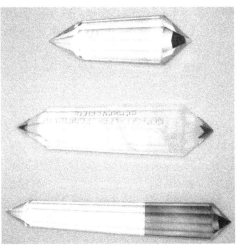

strong connection to the Spirit world and, as the story was told to me (although I cannot vouch for its accuracy) Jesus appeared to him and asked if he were willing to work for Higher good. Marcel Vogel agreed and intuitively was taught how to cut crystals to promote healing. In the picture of the three crystals, the top two are used for general purposes, while the third, a combination of clear and smoky quartz, is specifically designed for opening the throat chakra. Often we have been taught to hold back our truth, keep our emotions inside or swallow our feelings. Because of this the throat energy center, in most clients I see, is often blocked. *"The throat chakra is the bridge between the heart and the mind. If the throat is not open, the heart does not feel safe to be open."* (James Hughes) This means that if one is unable to express one's truth, the heart feels vulnerable to humiliation, criticism or other verbal/emotional attack and will not allow itself to be fully open to love. If the throat chakra is blocked, the mind will supersede the heart to keep the self safe through logic. When the throat chakra is open information between the heart and mind flows and allows for both heartfelt and logical information to be used harmoniously to bring perfect balance to life.

The remaining two photos are of a beautiful 100 lb deep purple

amethyst crystal geode and a view of some crystals under the grid bed. You can notice the crystal filled copper tubes in the foreground. These create a boarder under the bed that along with the crystals created an energy field conducive to centering and deepening one's connection to his/her own energy field. There is always energy going on around us and we are picking it up, hence the reason why we may feel uncom-fortable around people we don't resonate with or feel relaxed out in nature. The crystals create a field of natural energy that allows for deeper relaxation.

I would like to clarify that Alchemical/Spiritual Hypnotherapy may be successfully accomplished anywhere and without anything but a hypnotherapist skilled in the Alchemical Craft. I have given powerful sessions in many settings, including hotel rooms with noisy hallways. Using the crystals and energy grid bed is something that was brought into my life by Spirit through the physical form of James Hughes. I love and appreciate the crystals and enjoy working  with them. If you are interested in incorporating crystals in your work and would like high quality source for them, I would recommend contacting James and Rosemary Hughes *

* Contact James & Rosemary Hughes at: channels@ashlandoregon.org or by calling 541-488-2872

Glossary

These are my personal definitions for some of the words/concepts I have used in this book. I have no dispute with anyone who defines them differently.

Great Spirit, God/Goddess, God Source, Universal Intelligence, Universal Energy , Divine Energy - That which is part of everything and that which we are a part of. That which knows the *big picture* and That whose plan we are a part of.

Spirit/spirit - When capitalized I am speaking of the Great Spirit. In lower case, spirit may refer to the human soul or to any essence that is of the non-physical realm.

Spirit Guides - Those energies whose purpose is to guide us. These guides are personal and appear as angels, animals, elders, or whichever form best serves the one receiving guidance.

Soul - The spirit part of ourselves. That part which is made in the image and likeness of God. The soul is the part of ourselves that slips into a physical body each time we incarnate. The soul is our higher self and connects our physical being with the God Source.

Higher Self - Our soul self and our connection to the infinite wisdom of the God Source.

Future Pacing – a hypnotherapeutic technique that allows the client to take what has happened during the session and project it to a time in the future to find out how it will work.

Third Eye – also known as the inner eye, is the energy center of the crown chakra and associated with intuition, inner vision and clairvoyance.

Etheric Plane – That place where spirit lives

Readers are cautioned that his book is not intended to replace advice or treatment for any medical or emotional problems. In the event that you use any of the information in this book for yourself, the author and publisher assume no responsibility for your actions.

Contact the Author

For those of you interested in pursuing this work more deeply, or if you have questions, or comments, you may write to:

Linda Baker
1202 N. 35th Street,
Renton, Washington 98056-1964.
or email to: lindabak@hotmail.com

Also go to my Website: www.Innersourceseattle.com to read more articles I have written and find out more about what I do.

You can purchase the audiotape:

Abortion – A Spiritual Approach (this is the Spiritual Post-Conception work)

Side A: Abortion-A Spiritual Approach

Side B: Healing from Past Miscarriage/Abortion

by mailing a check for $15.00 to the above address.

The Alchemy Institute

If you are interested in pursuing comprehensive, spiritually based hypnotherapy as a career* or to add these skills to your current practice I highly recommend my teacher, David Quigley who is the Founder and Director of the Alchemy Institute.

You may reach him and find more information about the Alchemy Institute by writing, calling or emailing:

David Quigley
Alchemy Institute of Hypnosis
567-A Summerfield Rd
Santa Rosa CA 95405
(707) 537-0495
(800) 950-4984
info@alchemyinstitute.com
www.alchemyinstitute.com
David Quigley's private
practice: (707) 539-4989
CHT, CCHT and Alchemical
Hypnotherapy Programs
at the Alchemy Institute
include:

> Trance Induction and Post Hypnotic Suggestion
> Emotional Clearing Therapy
> Advanced Past Life Regression and Inner Guides
> Conference Room Therapy
> Specific Regimens
> Establishing a Professional Practice
> Advanced Electives include: Somatic Healing, Advanced Alchemical Techniques, Healing the Trauma of Sexual Abuse, Hypnosis with Children, Empowerment Intensives, Seminar Leadership, Magic Theatre and more.

*Personal transformation packages are available for those who do not seek professional credentials.

David Quigley created Alchemical Hypnotherapy in 1984 and has mentored the establishment of training centers around the world. Approved by the National Guild of Hypnotists (NGH) and by the California Board of Private Postsecondary and Vocational Education, the California Board of Registered Nursing and the California Board of Behavioral Sciences. CEU's are available for nurses, therapists, body workers, hypnotherapists, and others.

David Quigley Founder & Director of the Alchemy Institute

Write from the Heart

I encourage anyone who has an interest in writing, whether it be personal or for publication, to consider taking a:

Write From the Heart Seminar
with Hal Zina Bennett
For more information call 707-275-9011
Visit Hal's website at: www.HalZinaBennett.Com (Download Free Newsletters!)
or email Hal at: halbooks@pacific.net

Hal is dedicated to personal empowerment through self-expression and self-knowledge. His writing seminars are powerful, creative experiences that truly allow their students to write from the heart. Without Hal's teaching and support I doubt that Soul Contracts would have been written. If you are interested in writing, check out *Write From the Heart* and Hal's newest book: *Write Starts,* a handy resource for practiced and aspiring writers alike. *Write Starts* facilitates creativity like the perfect seat at a favorite café or a peaceful room of one's own. What's more, it puts you in the congenial company of a wise and expert coach.

Hal Zina Bennett
If you are interested in self-publishing I encourage you to contact iUniverse.com.

Linda Baker

Linda and her husband Tom, live in a rustic hunting lodge that was built in 1925 and overlooks Lake Washington and the Olympic Mountain Range. They have been blessed to live in this amazing location since 1974 and since that time have created a wonderful energy-center. They enjoy making their space available to those who come for workshops, healing sessions, or just to spend time in the crystal gardens.

Among other things, Linda, loves nature, gardening, writing, reading, growing spiritually, walking, running and spending loving time with Tom, children, grandchildren and dear friends. Besides her professional work, which brings her immense joy, Linda donates time in service to others.

Quan Yin ~ Goddess of Compassion, in the Crystal Garden

"I no longer try to change the outer things. They are simply a reflection. I change my inner perception and the outer reveals the beauty so long obscured by my own attitude. I concentrate on my inner vision and find my outer view transformed. I find myself attuned to the grandeur of life and in unison with the perfect order of the universe."

~ The Daily Word

Epilogue

As we look to heal the pain of our past, we find that love, is the only answer. Love allows us to see the big picture, to reach true forgiveness for ourselves and others and to open our hearts to gifts our bountiful Universe has for us. My life has been transformed through this work and I give thanks daily for the joy filled life that is mine. My intention in writing this book is to pass on what I have learned in hopes that you too will accept the challenge of delving into your inner world to release the beliefs and energy that no longer serve your highest good. I know that when you do this you will feel the love and grace of the Divine even more present in your daily life.

Buddha in the garden

CPSIA information can be obtained
at www.ICGtesting.com
Printed in the USA
FSHW01n1951240918
52513FS